Sᴡɪᴛᴢᴇʀʟᴀɴᴅ
BY TRAIN

Marianne Luka-Großenbacher

JPMGᴜɪᴅᴇꜱ

CONTENT

A clock CFF, keeping the trains punctual

stunning peaks

A beautifully decorated festive cow

ALL ABOARD, PLEASE!

Switzerland is a small country with a compact and efficient road network, yet what better way to explore its spectacular landscapes than by rail? In fact, the train is more relaxing and is often also quicker than travelling by road; for example, crossing the country from Basel to Lugano or from Geneva to St. Gall only takes 4 hours! What's more, the service is reliable and trains are frequent and usually on time.

Switzerland in a Nutshell

La Suisse, die Schweiz, la Svizzera, la Svizra. Switzerland has four languages—French, German, Italian and Romansch and many Swiss people also speak English, which they often master better than the other national languages.

With 7.8 million inhabitants, the Swiss Confederation, abbreviated CH from the Latin Confoederatio Helvetica, is divided into 23 cantons, three of which are split into half-cantons. The capital is Bern (pop. 135,000), while the biggest cities are Zurich (390,000), Geneva (193,000), Basle (190,000) and Lausanne (130,000).

With an area of 41,285 km^2 (15,935 sq miles), Switzerland is the most mountainous nation in Europe. The Alps cover 60% of the territory and the Jura mountain range covers another 10 %. This small region has a fascinating network of mountain trains. Here you can travel on the world's slowest Express train (the Glacier Express), the highest—and steepest—railway in Europe (the Bernina line) and visit Europe's highest railway station, inside the Jungfraujoch, alt. 3454 m. As you relax and climb 1,400 metres in 50 minutes, allow yourself to be dazzled by this amazing feat of engineering and the outstanding panoramic view. On some trains you can try fondue.

The trains are clean and comfortable with well adapted connections. If your destination can't be reached by rail, it will surely be serviced by the alternative methods of either boat or local bus (*car postal*).

A romantic trip in the nostalgic steam train of the Rhätische Bahn, which is over 100 years old.

Rhätische Bahn, Chur/Reinhard Fasching

First or second class?

The Swiss federal railways (SBB/CFF/FFS) are comprised of highly modern rolling stock. The formation of the trains varies depending on whether they are running on a regional network (RegioExpress) or the main lines (InterCity). First class cars are spacious and comfortable; second-class cars are nice but quite often crowded.

InterCity trains connect the countries' main cities. Those with only one floor have a "family area", whereas trains with two floors usually have an entire "family-car" with a slide and children's playground. On some lines there are first class "business-areas" with high-speed Internet access (there is a charge), as well as a "silent area" for those who wish to escape day-to-day agitation for a while and travel in peace. Depending on the route and formation of the train, you can have something to eat in the restaurant car or even choose to eat right at your seat, thanks to the Minibar service (see "The Hard Facts").

The panoramic cars which are described in the following pages all have a pleasing tendency towards comfortable seats, even in 2nd class. So, treat yourself to some extra space and settle back ready to enjoy a unique travelling experience!

Announcements

Announcements over the loudspeaker are generally made in French, German and English, and in certain cases also in Italian. Most often, the next stop will be announced a few minutes before the arrival in the station, giving you ample time to get ready for it. The electronic display panel on the platforms show the train's final destination as well as the main stops along the way and the configuration of the train.

All aboard!

This guide is divided into 8 chapters, which are arranged in a mostly geographical order. The colors of the chapters help to differentiate between the featured railroads. At the beginning of each chapter you can find information about the city of departure, before you embark on your rail adventure.

Begin your holiday...gently. Instead of taking a train, take a boat (CGN) from Geneva or Lausanne and discover the beauty of western Switzerland with its vineyard terraces stretching down to the shores of the Lac Leman. These vineyards have been UNESCO listed since 2007. The boat will eventually take you to Montreux, home station of the GoldenPass line and first starting-point of the Swiss mountain-railway systems.

A wonderful sight from above Lake Geneva; vineyards and Swiss alps.

LAKE GENEVA

Few areas of Switzerland have acquired such a flattering—if well-deserved—reputation as the Lake Geneva region. The combination of ever-changing lake, terraced vineyards and mountain backdrop is unique. What's more, thanks to an extremely efficient rail network, it is from here that you can set out to explore the heights of the country; south, north, east and west!

CGN – »All aboard!«

The lake forms a huge crescent, 72 km (45 miles) long, 14 km (8.5 miles) across at its widest point. Sixty percent of its area of 584 sq km (234 sq miles) belongs to Switzerland, the rest to France.

No fewer than 40 ports on the French and Swiss shores are served by the largest fleet of paddle-wheel boats in the world, managed by the *Compagnie générale de Navigation* (CGN).

Excursion boats ply the lake in all directions so you can, for example, board in Lausanne and travel to the Evian-les-Bains Spa in France.

Of its six graceful Belle Epoque paddle-wheelers, built between 1904 and 1927, five are powered by steam engines, and one by electric diesel engine. The fleet is completed by eleven modern ships and rapid launches called Navibus, which are principally used by commuters travelling between France and Switzerland for work.

Lausanne

Halfway along the north shore, Lausanne is a business, administrative and university centre, with a population of 130,000. It is built on many hills, which makes its layout confusing but delights skate-boarders who sweep down the slopes, oblivious to the traffic. The city rises in tiers from the port of Ouchy on the lake shore to the medieval cathedral in the old town.

Ouchy

With its parks, tree lined promenade, terraces, fountains and beautiful Alpine view, not to mention it's majestic, luxury hotels, Ouchy is a popular meeting place. Just next to the castle and opposite the metro station, a clock is charged with counting down the time remaining until the next winter and summer Olympic Games; the engraved pictographs represent various olympic sports.

Set in sculpture-dotted landscaped gardens, the **Olympic Museum** showcases the history of the famous games. Here you can view everything from the antique vase of Athena-Nikê to the Nikes of athlete Carl Lewis, or watch past sporting exploits on video. (Closed for renovation until the end of 2013.)

Next door, a stately mansion in expansive grounds houses the **Musée de l'Elysée**, devoted to photography.

Further east, in the **Parc du Denantou**, stands the gold-clad Thai pavilion, a gift to the city from King Bhumibol who attended school in Lausanne.

Thousands of years ago, there was a Gallo-Roman settlement at lake-level; the stone foundations of Lousonna have been laid bare at **Vidy**, west of Ouchy, where besides the Roman museum, you will find the Théâtre de Vidy, designed in 1964 by Max Bill, as well as a restaurant, sports complex and a small gravel beach. The big municipal beach, with several swimming pools, is between Ouchy and Vidy at Bellerive.

City Centre

Lausanne is the only Swiss town with a Métro. The **m2** line is the world's steepest, with a gradient of up to 12%. It links Ouchy and the centre with the north side of town. The **m1** line runs east-west from the centre (Flon) to the university district (EPFL, UNIL) and Renens.

Once serving as a place for storage and stock-turnover and left in a state of neglect, **Flon** is today a trendy quarter known for its vibrant night-life. Buildings of the most modern design now house shops, offices and bars. Today, only the pattern of the cubic structures recall the old industrial warehouse district.

Place Saint-François is the nerve centre of town, where all the

---

Olympic city. As home to the International Olympic Committee since 1915, and to the Olympic Museum opened in 1993, Lausanne likes to polish its sporting image by hosting an impressive number of top sports events such as Athletissima, and an international Beach Volley tournament. Runners get a work-out in the city's 20-km (12-mile) race and the Lausanne Marathon. There is also an annual swimming race across Lake Geneva. Since 2006 over 20 international sports federations have joined the International House of Sport.

buses meet. It is flanked by imposing banks and the monumental post office; in the middle stands the 13th-century **church of Saint-François**, on the site of a Franciscan monastery. A smart shopping street is the cobbled **Rue de Bourg**. Heading uphill, turn to the left into rue Caroline then cross the Pont Bessières to reach **la Cité**.

The Gothic **cathedral of Notre-Dame** was consecrated by Pope Gregory X in 1275, in the presence of Emperor Rudolf von Habsburg. A superb rose window survived the anger of the Reformation. On the south side, the "painted portal", showing traces of the original polychrome. A medieval tradition has been upheld—every night from 10 p.m. to 2 a.m., a watchman, the *guet*, calls out the hours from the tower. The former bishop's palace next to the cathedral is now the **Historical Museum of Lausanne**, with a fascinating scale model of the 17th-century walled town. Next door is the **Museum of Design and Contemporary Applied Arts (Mudac)**.

Among the narrow streets leading off from the north side of the cathedral you will find a few bars, boutiques, antiquarian and antique shops. Covered steps lead down from the esplanade to **Place de la Palud**, Lausanne's marketplace since medieval times. Overlooking the scene is the 17th-century **Hôtel de Ville** (Town Hall), with arches, clocktower, flower-filled window boxes and wrought-iron dragon gargoyles. People gather on the steps of the **Fountain of Justice** to watch and listen to the **animated clock** marking the hour with a parade of soldiers and historical figures illustrating the Vaudois battle for independence against the Bernese overlords.

On Wednesday and Saturday mornings, the fruit, flower and vegetable stalls spill over the square and on the first Friday of every month (March to November), local artisans sell their crafts in the Marché des Artisans-Créateurs on Place de la Palud and along neighbouring streets such as rue de la Madeleine and into **Place de la Riponne**, a large square presided over by the monumental **Palais de Rumine**. It houses several museums; perhaps the most interesting is the Musée des Beaux-Arts, which often stages special fine arts exhibitions.

Unique Museums

Northwest of the centre, opposite the exhibition halls of the Palais de Beaulieu, the unusual **Collection d'Art Brut** of Lausanne features French artist Jean Dubuffet's strange but compellingly beautiful collection of works in addition to works by unconventional, untrained artists such as prisoners or psychiatric patients.

The elegant 19th-century mansion **l'Hérmitage**, on the northern fringes of Lausanne, is the setting for temporary art exhibitions of note. There is a splendid view of the cathedral and the lake from the villa's gardens.

Vevey

The old Roman settlement of Vibiscus is today the capital of the Lavaux wine-growing region, and the headquarters of the multinational food company Nestlé. The town surrounds the vast **Grande Place** (market square), which opens onto the lake, In July and August, for the Saturday market, the stallholders don traditional costume and local wine flows freely. Another big market, St Martin's Fair, is held in November.

The Musée suisse de l'appareil photographique (photography museum) stands on one side of the Market Square; here you can trace the history of the camera from its birth to the digital era.

Round the corner along the lake front, a large and dignified mansion is home to the **Alimentarium**, an interactive food museum, with an emblematic sculpture of a giant fork in the lake. Nearby stands a bronze **statue of Charlie Chaplin**. The actor lived with his large family in the Manoir du Ban, in Corsier just above Vevey, from 1952 until

Confrérie Des Vignerons

Wine Festival. For years, the *Confrérie des Vignerons* has been organizing a wine festival in Vevey that has its documented origins in annual processions going back to 1647. From 1730 sculpted wooden figures were carried through the streets, honouring Bacchus and his horde and a few years later the harvest goddess Ceres joined the festivities. As the cost of the festival grew, it could be staged only every three to six years, but it developed as an important tradition, unique to Switzerland. From the end of the 18th century, the Fête des Vignerons, in addition to celebrating the traditional divinities of mythology, paid tribute to the work of the vineyards and the animals used in the harvest. For the occasion, eulogies, hymns and dances were created, along with special costumes. Given its elaborate staging, only 11 festivals have been held since 1797, the next is planned for the summer of 2019. In the **Musée de la Confrérie des Vignerons**, 2 Rue de Château in Vevey, you can get a close-up view of the Festival's splendours.

his death in 1977. It is planned to transform his house into a museum, **Chaplin's World** in 2014. Also on the lakefront is a monument to the Russian novelist **Nikolai Gogol**, who lived and worked in Vevey in 1836, and a bust of the Romanian poet **Mihail Eminescu**.

The recently renovated **Musée Jenisch**, on Avenue de la Gare, has a remarkable collection of Swiss and other artworks of the 19th and 20th centuries, ancient and modern drawings, etchings and engravings, as well as the works of the Kokoschka Foundation.

Walk beneath the trees in the direction of Montreux to La Tour de Peilz, where the 13th-century castle houses the **Musée Suisse du Jeu** (Toy Museum).

Funi to Mont-Pèlerin

From Vevey, take the Funiculaire which leaves from the west side of the train station, on Châtel St-Denis Road. The train climbs to an altitude of 810 m (2,654 ft). Near the top, in the village of Mont-Pèlerin, there are several hotels with spectacular views, gourmet restaurants as well as an interesting Buddhist study centre, which is usually open to spontaneous visitors.

You can then walk or drive to **Plein Ciel**, a panoramic elevator which rises to the top of the transmissions tower on the summit. From here there is an unparalleled view (open Easter to October).

Train to Chamby

Railway buffs will not want to miss the Blonay–Chamby line. A narrow-gauge electric train winds up from Vevey station to **Blonay** and its 12th-century castle.

On Sundays between the end of April and early October, a **historic museum train** leaving from there puffs up to Chamby (see www.blonay-chamby.ch).

The Chaulin-Chamby depot, accessible only by train, has one of Europe's biggest collections of metric-gauge railway carriages.

Train to the Pléiades

A cogwheel train leaves Vevey (or Blonay) for the Pléiades, culminating at 1,397 m (4,583 ft). Also known as the 'Train of the Stars', it's a fabulous trip to take.

The open-air exhibition park of AstroPléiades, (open from May to November) was designed with the help of wellknown Swiss astronaut Claude Nicollier. Its interactive exhibits include scale models of the universe and of the solar system. Children will no doubt be fascinated by this informative and absorbing park.

The area is popular with skiers in winter and hikers (you can hire a pair of Nordic walking poles at Blonay station) and hang gliders during the summer.

Montreux

The Belle-Epoque town of Montreux stretches out languidly along Lake Geneva, its buildings rising up in tiers, each window drinking in the view. Steep mountains shelter the town from chilly northeast winds. A 7-km (4-mile) lakeside promenade exploits its special micro-climate: all kinds of flowers and plants, even palm trees and bananas, thrive here, in a setting reminiscent of the French Riviera. Along the hushed corridors of palatial grand hotels you walk in the footsteps of Nabokov, Hemingway, Stravinsky, Lord Byron and Empress Elizabeth of Austria.

Montreux is a full-time international tourist resort, where something is always happening — an international conference, a music festival, a bustling Christmas market. July sees the prestigious **Montreux Jazz Festival** mapping the city's name all over the world, followed by festival of classical music in collaboration with the town of Vevey, the **September Musical**. A plethora of posh health spas and medical clinics are established, ideal for followers never getting old whiche benefit from Montreux's micro-climate.

At 40, Rue de la Gare, the **Musée de Montreux** (April to early November) documents the town's history. Most tourists congregate down on the flower-trimmed quays stretching from the modern Stravinski Auditorium and Centre des Congrès to the Casino and beyond. You'll spot statues of

Promenade fleurie. Among the countless attractions of the Riviera between Vevey and Montreux, one of the favourites for people of all ages is a walk along the quais, lined from one end to the other with planters full of colourful flowers. You can stroll (or run, skate or cycle) for some 10 km (except for a private stretch between La Tour de Peilz and Clarens), to Montreux and even further, past the castle of Chillon and Villeneuve at the eastern end of the lake. The gardeners of Montreux create a new series of stunning vegetal sculptures every year, set among the flowerbeds. Off Villeneuve you'll notice a tiny island, Ile de Peilz, just big enough for one tree. It was given to Queen Victoria but she graciously returned the gift to Switzerland a few years later.

istockphoto.com/Geer

many famous people as you walk around—Freddy Mercury near the covered market; a bust of Miles Davis near the Congress Centre; B.B. King, Ray Charles, Ella Fitzgerald, Aretha Franklin and Quincy Jones in the little park opposite the Montreux Palace, in the company of Nabokov in knickerbockers lolling back in his chair.

The impressive castle of Chillon, perched on a lakeside rock.

Château de Chillon

East of Montreux, on a small rocky promontory jutting into the lake stands the majestic castle of Chillon. A defensive military fortress and feudal ducal castle, it is one of the best-known landmarks of Switzerland and the most-visited historic site in the whole country.

Its origins are lost in the mists of time. The first fortress was built on the ruins of a Roman watchtower. The oldest parts of today's castle date back to the 11th century. In the middle of the 12th century, the counts and dukes of Savoy made it their main residence, expanding it several times. The castle's golden age was from the 13th to 14th centuries.

Its renown was revived in the 19th century when writers such as Victor Hugo, Alexandre Dumas and Lord Byron found inspiration in its mighty walls; Byron took it as the setting for his famous poem *The Prisoner of Chillon*, recounting the story of Bonivard, the 16th-century Geneva prior who tried to introduce the Reformation and was imprisoned by the Savoyards for his trouble. Touring the castle today, exploring its grand halls, its weaponry rooms and dungeons, is like taking a plunge into the Middle Ages. Plans are in place to restore the castle soon.

Le Bouveret

On the southeast shore of the lake, Le Bouveret has two sights worth visiting: an Aquaparc and the **Swiss Vapeur Parc** (mid March to end October).

The park covers an area of 17,000 sq m with miniature historic locomotive trains, steam ship models and small-scale versions of other Swiss tourist attractions.

Even the vineyards surrounding the small castle of Aigle appear to be scaled down to size.

Rochers-de-Naye

As you approach Montreux you will probably have noticed a blunt peak sticking up above the mountains like thumbs. This is the Rochers-de-Naye, culminating at 2,042 m (6,670 ft), the highest summit on the north shore of Lake Geneva. The area is popular with skiers in the winter, hanggliders during the summer and also with hikers. There are two restaurants perched here, one is close to the train station, the other is a panoramic restaurant which can be reached via a tunnel, and offers a splendid view. Don't miss the **Botanical garden** full of pretty Alpine plants. In the **Marmotte Paradis** are several species of cute little marmots from Switzerland, Russia, Uzbekistan and North America. If you want to spend the night, you can book a Mongolian yurt.

The most spectacular part of the trip, apart from the view from the (windy) summit, is the arrival. The narrow-gauge (80 cm) railway line, built in three stages around 1900, was, at the time, one of the steepest in the world.

Clinging to the slopes are the villages of **Glion** and **Caux**, the second with a huge turreted grand hotel now used as a conference centre. Austrian Empress Elizabeth (Sissi) stayed in Caux several times towards the end of the 19th century.

Chocolate Train

From May to October, on Monday, Wednesday or Thursday (and daily July–August), this special MOB train is a must for railway buffs, even more so if they are gourmets. You can ride in a panoramic car, or one of the Belle-Epoque Pullman cars supplied for the MOB in 1931. The train leaves Montreux for Montbovon and the **Gruyère region**, where the famous cheese is made, you can see the production at the **Maison du Gruyère**. This charming medieval town is perched high on a hill, enclosed by ramparts and guarded by a 15th-century castle, today a museum. In the nearby town of **Broc**, the Chocolate Train terminus, passengers can visit the **Maison Cailler** to see how chocolate is made—and taste it.

GoldenPass Line

The Montreux-Bernese Oberland line (MOB) was begun in 1901 with the stretch from Montreux to Les Avants; completed in 1905 with the line to Zweisimmen. The branch to La Lenk was inaugu-

---

GoldenPass (MOB): technical data

Type: narrow-gauge electric railway

Traction: adhesive/cog wheel

Length: 75,2 km (46,7 miles)

In service since: 1901–1905

Tunnels: 18

Bridges: 63

rated in 1912. In 1931, four prestigious Pullman cars owned by the *Compagnie Internationale des Wagons-Lits* were added to the rolling stock, but in face of the worldwide economic crisis the service was withdrawn soon. In 1976, international interest in this line was re-awakened.

From the first panoramic wagon to a complete panoramic train.

In 1976 the world's first panoramic coach (wagon) came into service, with three others following in 1979. In 1986, the first engine possessing a kind of panoramic cockpit was created to tow the train and ultra modern panoramic coaches have been in service since the year 2000, for both first and second class passengers. Three million passengers use the **GoldenPass Panoramic** yearly, or the **GoldenPass Classic** train with its first-class carriages dating from the Belle Epoque era of 1915. Departing from the shores of Lake Geneva the trains head for the Simmental, passing the Pays d'Enhaut and the Saanenland. You can continue to Lucerne, but will need to change in Zweisimmen and Interlaken.

Grandiose landscapes travelling with the GoldenPass Panoramic train. | A Gruyere cheese can weigh anywhere between 25 and 40 kg.

Goldenpass.ch

hemis.fr/Sudres

In the 19th century, the art of paper cutting was developed in Switzerland, especially in the Pays-d'Enhaut and the Saanenland.

On request, the MOB offers rides in engines of the 6000 or 8000 Class. To experience the journey from a different perspective, accompany a driver working on the train. Feel how the concentrated force of the railway engine pulls the whole train over the **Col de Jaman** and **Saanenmöser Passes**. This unforgettable experience is marked with a diploma and historical documentation about the Montreux-Bernese-Oberland line.

From Montreux to Zweisimmen

Have your camera ready; leaving Montreux, the GoldenPass Panoramic climbs up the north shore of the lake in a northwesterly direction, turning at Chernex to reveal a marvellous panorama of the lake and mountains.

Pays d'Enhaut

After the station of **Les Avants**, the train disappears into a tunnel boring deep into the mountain beneath the Dent de Jaman, emerging on the Gruyère side to enter the Pays-d'Enhaut, the western French-speaking part of the Saanenland, which belongs to Vaud canton.

In **Rossinière**, you ride past the mighty **Grand Chalet** with its 113 windows, home of the renowned Franco-Polish painter Balthus, who lived and worked here from 1977 until his death in 2001.

The main town in this green valley watered by the Sarine river and embraced by mountains is picturesque **Château-d'Œx**, a summer and winter resort known worldwide for the hot-air balloon competitions held every January.

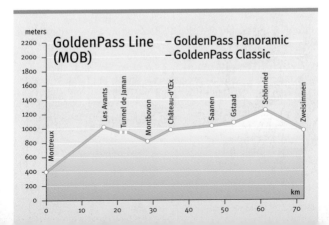

Not far from Château d'Oex, **L'Etivaz**, is renowned for its dairy, where a delicious tangy hard cheese, similar to Gruyère is made from the milk delivered from the region's alpine chalets.

Saanenland

In the region around the town of **Saanen** the national language changes from French to German. Classical music recitals are held in the lovely **parish church of Saint Maurice** (1447), which the violinist Yehudi Menuhin chose as the original venue for a music festival that has now grown into a seven-week event in several locations of the valley.

The undisputed star of the region is **Gstaad**, a popular resort for the international jet set. Initially the MOB would have bypassed Gstaad, but the inhabitants of Gstaad were persuaded that a 3-km detour was necessary; since then the people of Gstaad have never looked back. The emblem of the resort is the majestically turreted **Palace Hotel** (1912) towering over the village, which has retained its convivial atmosphere despite the number of celebrities who throng the streets. The accent is on discreet, even during the international tennis and polo tournaments. It's only when you start window-shopping that you notice from the price-tags that the clientèle is perhaps

on a different planet. A coffee and delicious treat from one of the patisseries whilst people watching and absorbing the atmosphere is a great way to pass an hour or two in the village centre.

From Gstaad you will reach Schönried and Saanenmöser, gateway to the Simmental. The area is garlanded with cable cars and ski lifts, making it one of the best skiing domains of the Bernese Oberland. After 17 km following the Petit Simme, the train will reach Zweisimmen, the main town of the Upper Simmental, where the rails of the MOB end. A branch line of the MOB links up to the holiday resort of **La Lenk** (1,068m), departure point for hikes or cross-country skiing. The Simme river has its source near Siebenbrunnen at the foot of the »Wildstrubel«.

Zweisimmen - Lucerne

In Zweisimmen, an ordinary train (standard gauge railway) will wait for passengers in transit for Lucerne. For this stretch, the saloon coaches 1st class are fitted with individual pivoting seats, enabling you to get a perfect view of the carved wooden chalets in the Simme valley.

Simmental and Lake of Thun

You will soon get a view of the **Schloss Blankenburg** and, a little further on, the old **wooden bridge** of

Boltigen. Here and there, castle ruins bear witness to the historic past of the Weissenbach barons. In **Erlenbach** you will find a folklore museum and a church with handsome paintings. Entrance and exit to the valley are guarded by the **Schloss Wimmis**. It is here that you may glimpse the typical Simmentaler cattle (p.2) in the valley's green pastures before it opens up to Spiez and Thun Lake where the route turns east towards Interlaken (p.27). Just on the right before Interlaken Ost the Jungfrau (4,158m) is visible.

From Interlaken to Lucerne

From Interlake Ost, you will pass Lake Brienz and the **Ballenberg Open-Air Museum** and then through the Hasli Valley towards Meiringen. From there the train tackles an altitude difference of 400m to level up with the **Brunig Pass** (1,008m). If you have time, it is worth making an excursion to **Hasliberg**, an extensive sunny platform with a splendid view over the Bernese Alps.

The descent to Lucerne is 43km long, with an altitude difference of 600 m. You quickly leave the canton of Bern behind and the Obwalden canton welcomes you with the picturesque **Lake Lungern** and the church of Giswil. On the eastern bank of **Lake Sarner**, before reaching the village of Sarnen and nestled in

www.stanserhorn-bahn.ch

Cabrio-Bahn, the world's newest cable car–with an outside view!

the hills to the right of Sachseln is **Flüeli-Ranft**, the hermitage of **Niklaus von Flue** (Brother Klaus).

A little further on are Alpnach and Alpnachstad with the valley station of Pilatusbahn (p.38). On the opposite valley side looms the Stanserhorn. Since June 2012 a state-of-the-art aerial cable car with an open-air deck, the **Cabrio-Bahn**, has led to the summit. It leaves from Stans between April and November. Hergiswil is close to the lake (p.35) and canton of Lucerne; the capital is only several kilometres away (p.33).

Man's best friend? St. Bernards are traditionally bred as mountain rescue dogs in the Swiss Alps.

Martigny

In the elbow of the river, where the Rhône takes a right turn to flow towards Lake Geneva, the ancient city of Martigny (called Octodurus in Roman times) nestles among vineyards and wooded hills. Celts and Romans recognized this strategic location at the foot of the Alpine passes leading to Northern Italy and Savoy, and they set up military and trading posts there.

Red and white trains are awaiting you at the Martigny **station**. The emblems which can be seen on the carriages speak for themselves: Swiss crosses and three-coloured flags. The Mont-Blanc Express is headed straight for the Haute-Savoie Alps. On the Swiss side, it belongs to TMR SA (Transports de Martigny et Régions).

Boasting an image of the popular dog, the Saint-Bernard Express (property of RegionAlps SA) and a bus will get you to the Great St Bernard Pass. Before you embark on your railroad journey, stop at one of the cafés on the beautiful **central square**, with its 19th century **town hall**. You can also hike up to the ruins of the **fort of Bâtiaz** (13th century), which used to dominate the city. Heading back down, on the right bank of the Dranse river, visit the **Fondation Luis Moret**, with its exquisite works of art. The **Manoir de la Ville**, a building from the 19th century at the heart of town, is a meeting point and stages contemporary art exhibitions.

Located to the southwest of the town centre (Rue du Forum), the **Fondation Pierre Gianadda** is renowned worldwide for its temporary exhibitions of great artists as well as for its permanent collections. This futuristic looking museum was built over the foundations of a Gallo-Roman temple, discovered in 1976. Antique archeological pieces are on display at the *Gallo-Roman museum*. The *Collection Franck* comprises works by Van Gogh, Picasso and other great masters. Further attractions include the splendid collection of old-timers at the *Musée de l'Automobile* and the *Parc des Sculptures*.

Starting at Fondation Gianadda, a path leads you to more archeological excavations as well as a Roman **amphitheatre**. Several cultural events take place in the renovated arena, such as the famous fights between the Hérens local cows in the autumn.

The **Musée et Chiens du Saint-Bernard** is nearby, at the old arsenal. You can admire these lovely dogs in outside enclosures and on the first floor you can learn more about the history of the St Bernard Pass and the hospice, founded in the Middle Ages.

Mont-Blanc Express

This cross-border line connects Martigny and Chamonix before reaching the station of Saint-Gervais-Le Fayet, 19km further westwards and part of the French TGV network (Rhône-Alpes).

The line's construction is the result of a daring project started at the end of the 19th century. Already around this time the **Mont-Blanc**, being the highest peak in the Alps at 4810m, attracted many mountaineers and tourists. In both Haute-Savoie and Valais the decision was made to serve this region with a better transport system. In 1901, the French started to build the first section and in Switzerland the works

began a year later. The engineers chose the untamed valley of Trient for the route. Years later, the railroad was used to dispatch construction material to the building-sites of the Barbedine (1925) and Vieux Emosson (1955) dams. Lastly, the Emosson dam (1975) was built, submerging the Barbedine in 42m of water.

Mont-Blanc Express: technical data
Type: narrow-gauge electric railway
Traction: adhesive + cog wheel
Length (to the frontier):
18,3 km (11.4 miles)
In service since: 1906
Tunnels + Galleries: 22 / **Bridges:** 28

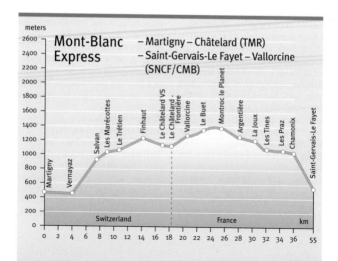

Trient Valley

In Vernayaz, the train starts to climb up the rock that bars the Rhône valley to the south. The 20% slope right before the village of Salvan is overcome thanks to a rack system and an electric power-supply that runs over a live rail.

The little holiday village of **Marécottes** is the entry point of the **La Creuzas** ski-slopes. Its tiny alpine zoo attracts many visitors. Between Marécottes and Finhaut, the rails cling to the cliffs, high above the **gorges of Triège** and **Trient**. The rails run through tunnels and galleries and cross several bridges and viaducts. **Finhaut** has beautiful paths for walking.

The attractions of the Châtelard

One kilometre before the border, disembark at Le Châtelard (the train will only stop at this station on demand) where three spectacular rail experiences await. Here you will become aware of the huge amount of effort and infrastructure that were needed to build a dam at the beginning of the twentieth century. The Martigny-Châtelard line was just the beginning.

The **CFF Châtelard museum** recounts the story of how the service had to produce their own electricity after the First World War.

The queen of Swiss Alpine flowers, the Eidelweiss is protected by law.

istockphoto.com / x-drew

Within a few minutes, the world's steepest **funicular rail** (87%) brings you from 1120m to 1822m of altitude, to a place called Les Montuires. This line is currently closed for renovation work and will reopen in 2014.

From there, the **panoramic Petit Train** (Little Train), with its open carriages, runs on Decauville narrow-gauge tracks (60cm wide) along the hillside for about 2km before reaching the foot of the Emosson dam. Towards the

---

Dam of Emosson:
Joint French–Swiss venture
Construction: 1969–1973
First use : 1975
Large lock barrier: 180 m
Content of the lake: 227 Mio. m³
Mean gross head : 1400 m
Total Production : 870 GWh,
250 in summer and 620 in winter

end, the **tiny funicular** climbs a 240m long slope at a 73% inclination to reach the station of **Lac d'Emosson**, located above the crown of the dam. A breathtaking panorama of the Mont-Blanc is revealed during the climb. A five-hour non-stop, round trip walk leaving from the railway station takes you beyond the Vieux-Emosson dam to **dinosaur footprints** in the rock that are 250 million years old. From here you can take a bus back to Finhaut and climb back on board the Mont-Blanc Express, continuing your journey towards Chamonix or Martigny.

Hydroelectric power. Thanks to its topography and relatively high precipitation levels, Switzerland offers ideal conditions for hydroelectric power. Some 56% of Switzerland's generated electricity is derived from over 550 larger and smaller hydroelectric plants (plants producing at least 300kW) fed by reservoirs and rivers, producing 35,830 gigawatt hours annually. Almost half of this power is produced in river power stations. The proportion of power produced in pumped-storage hydropower plants is just 4%. The biggest hydroelectric power plant is the Grande Dixence in the canton of Valois. The mountain cantons of Uri, Graubünden, Ticino and Valois, together constituting part of the Gotthard Region, are responsible for two-thirds of hydroelectric production. In addition, the Aargau and Berne cantons make important contributions. International hydroelectric plants set on bodies of water at the frontier produce more than 10% of Switzerland's hydroelectric energy. The significance of hydroelectric power is evident in the fact that it represents 97% of the country's renewable energy.

Source: www.bfe.admin.ch

fotolia.com/JSummersgraphicsinc

Saint-Bernard Express

The name of the Saint-Bernard Express is symbolic rather than geographical. Although it was planned to build a railway line through the Grand-Saint-Bernard Pass in the 1850s, the project was not completed because the technical problems were insurmountable. However, a second line was opened in Martigny in 1910. A British company intended to build an aluminium plant at Orsières and financed the line to carry supplies. The plant never materialized, but the railway was still laid out along the Dranse, a tributary of the Rhône, to Sembrancher then Orsières (Entremont valley).

Grand-Saint-Bernard

Comfortably settled in one of the modern trains, you get a good view of the outskirts of Martigny before entering a landscape of fields, forest neat little villages and the last vineyards. The terminus is the pretty village of **Orsières**, where you transfer to a coach with the image of Barry, the famous Saint-Bernard dog who saved, thanks to his exceptional flair, many people who were lost or buried under the snow.

The bus takes you up to the **Hospice** of the Grand-Saint-Bernard Pass. It was founded in the 11th century to provide accommodation for travellers and is still inhabited by a handful of Augustinian monks. The small **Hospice Museum of Grand-Saint Bernard** documents the history of the Pass and its flora and fauna. In summer you will find the St Bernard dogs close to the hospice but they are kept down in the valley in Martigny during the winter.

Train to Le Châble

In 1953, a branch line 6 km (4 miles) long was built between Sembrancher and Le Châble, to carry construction materials for the Mauvoisin dam. The line is now used to take tourists to the cable cars serving the chic and popular ski resort of Verbier.

Bus lines from Orsières

At the foot of La Breya, **Champex-Lac** (1500m) is a summer holiday destination on the shore of a small, idyllic lake. The Alpine garden, **Flore-Alpe**, contains more than 4,000 species of plants from all over the world. You can also take a bus to **La Fouly** in the romantic and wild **Val Ferret**. It is a real paradise for hikers and mountain climbers.

Saint-Bernard Express: technical data
Type: standard gauge electric railway
Traction: adhesive
Length (to Orsières): 18,7 km (12 miles)
In service since: 1910
Tunnels/Galleries: 10
Bridges: 26

The pure art work evident in the carving and colours of these chalet façades in Berner Oberland is eyecatching.

Interlaken

One of the most sensational experiences in Switzerland is the train ride up to the Jungfraujoch, which boasts the highest railway station in Europe at 3,454 m (11,332 ft). No overseas tourist would dream of missing out this top destination. Japanese signposts are just one sign of Interlaken's international appeal.

Interlaken Traffic Junction

Its location on the Bodeli east of the lively Lake Thun and west of turquoise-blue Lake Brienz explains the town's name, Interlaken, "between two lakes". Already, at the turn of the 20th century, tourists flocked to the grand hotels along the Hoheweg, the town's prestigious promenade. Interlaken is the junction of various travel routes offering excursions in different directions by boat or by train.

The renowned open-air Interlaken **Tell Plays** are staged here from late June to early September. Written by Schiller, they relate the story of Guillaume Tell and the legendary acquisition of Swiss independence (speeches are delivered in German). In the nearby **Jungfrau Park**, there is much to be learned about the mountain world and children can enjoy a great variety of attractions. Anybody taking the **Two Lake Cruise** has to change in Interlaken as the

Aare Canal is too narrow for the ships to pass through. It is worthwhile taking a **Lake Brienz journey through time** with a steam boat, and private cable car which collects guests from the boat and takes them to the **Giessbach Grand Hotel.**

Via Brienz, you can also reach the **Ballenberg Open-Air Museum** open from mid-April to late October). Visitors here experience "Switzerland as it once was" with 100 buildings from the 16th to the 19th century from every region in the country, demonstrations of traditional crafts, and over 200 farm animals.

Back in **Interlaken Ost Station** you may catch a glimpse of the GoldenPass Panoramic on its way to Lucerne. But the undisputable highlight of all excursions here is the highly popular train journey to the Jungfraujoch.

Schynige Platte. From end May to end October, an old-fashioned wooden cog-wheel train goes up from Wilderswil to the Schynige Platte, first through thick forest then 1,500 m (4,921 ft) higher for a fabuous view of the Eiger, Mönch and Jungfrau, with Lake Thun sparkling down below. At the top you can browse around a small Alpine garden.

The valley of Lauterbrunnen, or 'The Valley of 72 Waterfalls'.

Huber/Ripani

Berner- Oberland-Bahnen BOB and Wengernalpbahn WAB

There are two ways of getting to Kleine Scheidegg, both taking about 75 minutes: at Zweilütschinen, one route heads off eastwards through the Lütschental to Grindelwald, the other goes south through the Lauterbrunnen Valley to the resort of Lauterbrunnen.

The two mountain villages, both of them popular sports resorts in winter and summer alike, could be reached by rail as far back as 1890, when the narrow-gauge lines were inaugu-

rated by the Berner Oberland-Bahnen (BOB). Three years later, the resorts were linked by the Wengernalp-Bahn (WAB), a line passing through the Kleine Scheidegg mountain pass, at 2,061 m (6,762 ft). This means, in effect, that you can arrange a circular trip, each branch of the railway having its own particular charms.

Via Wengen to Kleine Scheidegg

The train first crosses the Interlaken plain, with the Lake Brienz to the east and the Lake Thun to the west. Between Wilderswil and Zweilütschinen, the landscape changes as you pass steep cliffsides and enter the Lauterbrunnen Valley. At Lauterbrunnen station you change trains, leaving the BOB for the WAB.

If you have the time, before the climb to Wengen, it is worth making a side trip over to the **Trümmelbach Falls.** Ten glacier waterfalls in the interior of the mountains were made accessible and illuminated via a tunnel lift, stairs and galleries. The Trummelbach draws its water from the gigantic glacier walls of the Eiger, Monch and Jungfrau–up to 20,000 litres of water per second crash down the steep cliffs.

From **Lauterbrunnen** at 796m, the WAB rack railway meanders over bridges and viaducts, through tunnels and galleries to Wengen, set on a ledge at 1,274m

(4,180 ft). The panorama unfurls untold splendours, from the Staubbach waterfall opposite Lauterbrunnen to the grandiose backdrop of the Jungfrau massif.

Nestling at the foot of the Männlichen, 2,230 m (7,316 ft), and the Lauberhorn, 2,472 m (8,110 ft), where the famous ski race is held, **Wengen** is a traffic-free holiday resort popular summer and winter alike. The train continues further past hotels, handsome chalets and pastures green, climbing up to the resort of Wengernalp. On the last stage of the journey to the Kleine Scheidegg, you'll notice that the passengers automatically turn their gaze to the right. Towering high above, so close you could almost reach out and touch, is the most famous trio of the Bernese Alps: the Eiger, 3,970 m (13,025 ft), the Mönch, 4,099 m (13,449 ft) and the Jungfrau, 4,158 m (13,642 ft).

Via Grindelwald to Kleine Scheidegg

On the leg between Zweilütschinen and Grindelwald you stay on the BOB to ride through the narrow valley of the Lütschental. **Grindelwald** is a picture-postcard Alpine resort nestling among flower-filled meadows in summer and snow-capped peaks in winter.

From here you can board the WAB to Grindelwald-Grund;

after a steep climb the line makes a wide curve that brings you to the foot of the Eiger, continuing to the Kleine Scheidegg. In addition to the superb view on the far side of the valley, the most impressive thing about this trip is the imposing and almost crushing presence of the north face of the Eiger.

Kleine Scheidegg

The Kleine Scheidegg is a paradise for skiers in winter and for hikers and mountain climbers in summer. The most experienced mountaineers attempt the dangerous north face of 1600m of the Eiger. The record speed for its conquest stands at a breathtaking 2 hours 38 minutes. It was achieved by the Swiss mountaineer Daniel Arnold in 2011. The first recorded ascent in 1938 took three days.

Every April, the Snow Open Air Festival draws music lovers to its outdoor concerts and in September, the town is the arrival point of the famous Jungfrau Marathon.

Jungfraubahn: technical data
Type: narrow-gauge electric railway
Traction: cog wheel
Length: 9,3 km (5.8 miles)
In service since: 1912
Tunnels: 2

Jungfraubahn

Before you board the Jungfrau-Bahn (JB) train at Kleine Scheidegg, take a deep breath and fill your lungs, for soon the air will be so rarefied you will have to move slowly and avoid any unnecessary physical effort. In 1889 the pioneering construction plans of the JB were presented. By 1896 all the technical problems had been resolved, and the first ground was broken at the Kleine Scheidegg. Sixteen years later, on August 1,1912 and after multiple setbacks, Europe's highest railway station, at an altitude of 3,454 m (11,332 ft), was opened —the **Top of Europe**. The Jungfrau train takes about 50 minutes to travel through the Eiger and Mönch mountains, climbing some 1,400 m (4,593 ft) in all.

After leaving the lower station at 2,061 m (6,762 ft), the train climbs a slope with a gradient of 25%, then, after passing through an avalanche gallery and tunnel, reaches the **Eigergletscher Station**—(Eiger Glacier), at 2,320 m (7,611 ft). This is the site of the train maintenance workshop. The station is also the starting point of the **Eiger Trail**, taking you in 2–3 hours to Wart, a lookout point at the foot of the north face, and on to Alpiglen.

Continuing your journey, after Eigergletscher you will see nothing but rock, for the train enters a tunnel 7.12 km (over 4 miles) long, emerging only at the summit. But the engineers have thought of everything: from the glassed-in lookout of the **Eigerwand** or Eiger Wall, 2,864 m (9,396 ft) you enjoy a close-up view of the famous north face. On a fine day, you can see right over Grindelwald to the Lake Thun, perhaps even to the Jura and the Black Forest.

The next stop is at the **Eismeer**, Sea of Ice, 3,158 m (10,361 ft)

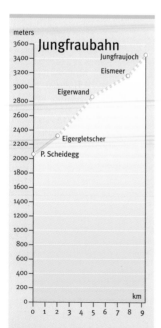

where you will spot, through the east-facing panoramic bay window, the glaciers of Grindelwald and Fiesch, as well as the Schreckhorn massif.

Soon afterwards, the train pulls into the **Jungfraujoch** station, carved entirely out of rock. Signs point to the circuit that was partly renewed for the 100-year Jubilee. In the Spinx-Hall, visit the **360 degree screen panoramic cinema** with its magnificent photography of the glaciers. Then take the elevator to the **International Station of Apine Research** with its observatory on the Sphinx cliff. The majestic Jungfrau-Aletsch natural park, listed as a UNESCO World Heritage site, the powerful Aletsch glacier and the arc of the Valais Alps all spread away in a breathtaking view from the terrace at your feet.

To the north the view extends over the Kleine Scheidegg to Interlaken and deep into the interior. On a clear day, you can take in an amazing view of 200 peaks.

Continue to the 250 m **Alpine Sensation Gallery**. Opened in 2012 it provides a direct link between the Sphinx Hall and the Ice Palace. Striking pictures, lighting and musical effects illustrate the history of tourism in the Jungfrau region, the grand idea of the visionary railway-builder Adolf Guyer-Zeller and the construction of the railway itself.

Jungfraubahnen

The 'Top of Europe' with panoramic views from the Sphinxfelsen.

At last you reach the **Ice Palace**, a great hall sculpted directly into the ice 20 m (65 ft) beneath the surface of the glacier. Shimmering blue ice sculptures of penguins and polar bears inhabit alcoves along the corridors. If you fancy a drink or more, there are several restaurants at hand to choose from.

The Jungfraujoch straddles the border between the Bern and Valais cantons, and is waiting to be explored. Visitors can ski or snowboard, go dog-sledding or take a guided walk on the glacier.

Chapel Bridge has long been a well-known landmark of Lucerne.

Lucerne

The geographical heart of Switzerland, described by Alexandre Dumas as "a pearl in the world's most beautiful oyster", Lucerne is an undeniably magical city. It sits on the shores of the Vierwaldstättersee (literally, the Lake of the Four Forest Cantons), the cradle of the Confederation, at the place where the lake narrows to form the fast-flowing River Reuss. The region is associated with William Tell, the famous patriot who stood up to the Habsburgs and for his temerity was forced to shoot an apple off his small son's head.

From the railway station you have an overall view of the lake and mountains and the city. The modern building you see behind the station, with a striking copper-clad roof, is the **KKL** – Lucerne's Culture and Convention Centre (1998), designed by the French architect Jean Nouvel. Its concert hall has stunning acoustics. On the 4th floor is Lucerne's **Art Museum** exhibiting Swiss artworks from the Renaissance to the present day.

The **Rosengart Museum** (Pilatusstrasse 10) west of the railway station highlights the works of Picasso, Klee and other modern and impressionist painters.

Out on the Tribschen promontory south-east of the station, the town has honoured one of its most celebrated visitors with the **Richard Wagner Museum**. The composer (1813–83) paid five visits to the city of Lucerne, working on his operas Siegfried, Tristan und Isolde and Götterdämmerung. Wagner, was moved to declare in a letter to King Louis II from Bavaria, "The sweet warmth of Lucerne's quay is such that it even makes me forget my music!"

Over the river you'll see the landmark **Kapellbrücke** (Chapel Bridge), one of the oldest wooden bridges in Europe (around 1330). With its eight-sided stone tower, the Wasserturm served as part of the town's fortifications and was used as a prison up till the 19th century. In 1993, the covered bridge was destroyed in a fire (not for the first time), but it has been reconstructed, and some of the 110 paintings on wood between the roof beams restored.

A little further along on the left bank, the **Jesuitenkirche** is one of the earliest and most beautiful baroque buildings in Switzerland. The simpler **Franziskanerkirche** is a charming contrast to baroque and Renaissance pomp. Built originally in high-Gothic style around 1300, the church boasts a richly carved wooden pulpit and choir stalls.

Cross the river at the **Spreuerbrücke**. This early 15th-century wooden bridge is colourfully ornamented with 67 murals, representing "Dance of Death" murals, painted between 1625 and 1632.

The **Mühlenplatz** leads into the Weinmarkt. This was Lucerne's thriving hub in the Middle Ages, crowded with guildhouses, shops and prosperous homes. Its elaborately painted façades still make this spot the most striking part of the Old Town.

The next square, the **Kornmarkt**, was the town's medieval corn distribution centre. The **Rathaus** (Town Hall), an impressive 17th-century building in stone. The Kornmarkt leads to what was in fact the hog market, now bedecked with flags, but named **Hirschenplatz**, after the old Gasthof zum Hirschen (Stag Inn) that was a favourite even in 15th century.

Make your way now up one of the pretty streets leading to the **Museggmauer**. This wall with its nine towers was built around 600 years ago to protect the city, it remains one of the best-preserved and longest wall fortifications in Europe. In season, you can visit the Clock Tower.

Northeast from the wall brings you to the heroic **Löwendenkmal**, the Lion of Lucerne was hewn from the rockface and designed by the Danish sculptor Thordvaldsen in memory of the Swiss Guards who perished defending the Tuileries in Paris in 1792.

Nearby is the **Gletschergarten**, an attractive park pock-marked with glacial potholes left by last remnants of the retreating ice age 15–20,000 years ago. The **Bourbaki Panorama** is a huge circular painting by Edouard Castres depicting an episode from the 1870–71 Franco-German war.

Towards the lake stands the elegant Hofkirche (Abbey Court Church). Note the façade's Tuscan-style arches and the two slim towers dating back to the 14th century. The richly carved choir stalls and the beautiful chancel screen inside were carved in the mid-17th century.

From here, the quay, lined with handsome hotels, leads east to the **Historic Seebad** (lakeside bathing establishment), popular with summer guests for its rooftop sunbathing. Further on is one of the best known Swiss museums, the **Verkehrshaus** (Transport House), whose exhibits display everything to do with transportation, from the old electric tram through to space capsules. Children love to take a ride on the miniature steam train.You will also find the country's largest planetarium here in addition to Switzerland's biggest film screen (508 sq m).

On the grounds of the Verkehrshaus is the **Hans Erni Museum**, documenting 7 decades of the renowned Lucerne artist's acti-

SCHIFFFAHRTSGESELLSCHAFT VIERWALDSTÄTTERSEE (SGV)

The SGV cruise company (Schifffahrtsgesellschaft Vierwaldstätter See) offers a unique nature experience amidst the splendid mountain world of central Switzerland. The lake stuns visitors with its dreamlike landscape, pine forests and formidable mountains. The highly active SGV has a fleet of ten different motor boats and five meticulously restored steamships. The oldest, the Uri, began service back in 1901. The newest ship, the elegant Saphir Panorama Yacht, was launched in 2012. They glide past neat little resort towns and history-laden Treib, Schillerstein, Tellskapelle and Rütli.

You are discovering the cradle of Switzerland's story. The valley stations of the mountains famous for their view—Pilatus and Rigi—are also accessible by ship. The William Tell Express begins its journey in Lucerne on an old-fashioned steam boat or motor boat and sails as far as Flüelen. From there, you continue in the first-class panorama coach along the Urn Reuss Valley towards Gotthard beyond Locarno and Lugano. Cruises with tempting culinary themes offer pastry or fondue menus, as well as a Sunday brunch and many other choices.

vity with 300 artworks. Make your way back to the station via the busy **Schwanenplatz**, but before crossing the Seebrücke, notice the romantic towered house on the corner of the bridge. The **Haus zur Gilgen** was named after the ambitious knight who built it in the 15th century.

Rigi Bahnen

Called the Queen of Mountains, Rigi stands in majesty opposite Lucerne, culminating at Rigi Kulm, 1,800 m (5,500 ft). There are several ways up to the top.

Vitznau-Rigi Cogweel Train

Take the steamboat from Lucerne for Vitznau, departure point for

Rigi Bahnen: technical data
Type: standard-gauge electric railway
Traction: electric + cog wheel + steam
Length: 7 km and 8.5 km
(4.3 and 5.2 miles)
In service since: 1871
Tunnels: 1 and 2 / **Bridges:** 7 and 8

Europe's very first mountain train. This cogwheel railway was the brainchild of Niklaus Riggenbach, who was decried by his fellow countrymen and had to go to France to get his invention patented. The canton of Lucerne granted him a concession, and in 1871 the stretch of line from **Vitznau** to Staffel, on the frontier with the canton of Schwyz, was inaugurated under the name Vitznau Rigi-Bahn (VRB). Two years later Riggenbach obtained permission from the Schwyz authorities to continue the 7-km (4-mile) line to the summit.

You may like to stop at **Rigi Kaltbad**, well known for its mineral springs since the 16th century. Treat yourself to a bracing pause in the imposing health resort of the **Mineralbad & Spa**, designed by Ticino architect Mario Botta and opened in 2012. There is a famous playground for children and numerous outdoor activities in summer and winter.

From July to September, a steam train runs the Goldau-Rigi-

meters

Vitznau-Rigi-Bahn

Rigi Kulm
Rigi Staffel
Rigi Staffellhöhe
Rigi Kaltbad-First
Romili Felsentor
Freibergen
Grubisbalm
Mittlerschwanden
Vitznau

km

Vitznau route, and on Sundays in the direction Vitznau-Rigi-Goldau. Reservation is recommended. Among the rolling stock, the RB owns several **Historic passenger coaches**, including No. 2 built in 1871, with open sides; No 11, built in 1889 with wrought-iron railings and known as "Bamboo"; the yellow-painted No. 35, a "third-class" carriage in service since 1899; and the luxurious Belle Epoque saloon coach (1873) in mahogany and brass with velvet upholstery.

If you have some extra time in Vitznau take a short walk to visit the once very secret artillery stronghold. Carved entirely out of rock, it was a military base during the second world war. Today it hosts a hotel for those fascinated by its design and history.

Arth-Rigi-Cogweel Train
In 1875, he tackled the mountain from the other side and built an 8.5-km (5-mile) rack railway from Arth on the shores of Lake Zug to Goldau and up to Rigi Kulm via Goldau (ARB). At Rigi-Klosterli, half-way up, is the small **Pilgrim chapel of Mary of the Snow**.

Between Staffel and Rigi Kulm, the train circles its route parallel to that of the VRB. Following years of fierce competition the two lines finally merged in 1992 to form the Rigi-Bahnen.

fotolia.com/Etzold

Alphornbläser playing the traditional Swiss Alphorn.

The stretch from Arth to Goldau was replaced by a bus service in 1959.

Aerial Cableway Weggis-Rigi Kaltbad
Another alternative is to get off the Lucerne boat at Weggis (a 45-minute trip) and take the panoramic cableway from Weggis up to Rigi Kaltbad. Inaugurated in 1998 it manages the 900 m dénivelation in a mere 10 minutes. During the summer, and only on demand, the cable car can even be transformed into an open air restaurant. In Rigi Kulm there are several hotels and restaurants. Once in Rigi Kaltbad you can change and board the Vitznau train for the last three stops. It is well worth taking time to visit the thermal baths here but if this doesn't really appeal then you can enjoy choosing your prefered mode of travel; boat, train or bus, to take you back to Lucerne.

Pilatus Bahnen

The Pilatus mountain has always been shrouded in mystery, its name attributed to Pontius Pilate. A popular myth related that Pilate's body was thrown into a lake west of the summit, and that he reappeared every Good Friday. Anyone who had the misfortune to encounter the apparition died during the following year. This belief was so strong that the mountain was placed out of bounds until 1585 when the Lucerne authorities had the lake dried up. A more prosaic explanation for the name is that it comes from the Latin for "in the clouds". Whatever, the mysterious aspect of the mountain is now exploited by the Pilatus railways (Pilatus-Bahnen) who fearlessly proclaim that "here be dragons". Well you're likely to encounter one, at least, and he's quite friendly especially towards children; his name is PILU®.

Cogweel Train
Alpnachstad-Pilatus Kulm

The **Pilatus Bahn** is described as the steepest train in the world — and though it looks like a funicular, it is indeed a train.

To reach **Alpnachstad**, catch the boat in Lucerne, pier No. 2 near the railway station (a 90-minute trip) or the train, which gets there in 20 minutes. From here to Pilatus Kulm at 2,132 m (7,000 ft) this little red Pilatus train is hauling itself up the 48% gradient by rack and pinion. Designed by Eduard Locher, the railway took three years to build and was inaugurated in 1889. It was opened by steam until 1937, when the 4.6-km narrow gauge line was electrified. The train does not run from mid November to mid May. After a trio of tunnels in quick succession you finally pull into the top

Pilatusbahn: technical data:
Type: narrow-gauge (80 cm) electric railway
Traction: cog wheel
Length: 4.6 km (2.8 miles)
In service since: 1889 / **Tunnels:** 5

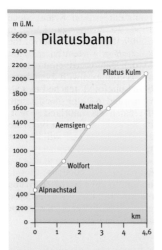

m ü.M.

Pilatusbahn

Pilatus Kulm
Mattalp
Aemsigen
Wolfort
Alpnachstad

km

The Pilatusbahn, travelling at incredible angles, is the steepest train line in the world.

station, beneath the round **Hotel Bellevue** and its neighbour the **Hotel Pilatus Kulm** (which was built before the railway). The latest infrastructure on Pilatus Kulm is a panoramic gallery between the two hotels. Complete renovation in 2010 marked a new chapter in the history of Mount Pilate, and the construction efforts of the railway company in creating the Pilatus Bahnen were officially recognised when it received the Milestone tourism prize in 2011.

A track leads from behind the Hotel Bellevue to the top of the **Esel peak**, 2,118 m (6,953 ft), for a 360° view over six lakes, over the Alpine range and as far as the Black Forest. A 35-minute walk to the **Tomlishorn** takes you to the Echoloch (echo chamber) and the finally the peak at 2,138 m (7,000 ft) overlooking the Vierwaldstättersee (Four Cantons Lake).

You can enter the **Drachenweg** (Dragon Path), a gallery cut through the mountain taking you in a 10-minute circuit. Hans Erni, a wellknown Swiss artist, has illustrated the gallery inspired by dragon myths and legends. A longer route, taking about half an hour, goes to the **Chriesiloch**.

Aerial Cableway
Pilatus Fräkmüntegg

For the return journey to Lucerne, you can take the cableway to **Fräckmüntegg** at 1,416m (4,649 ft).

This is the start of Switzerland's longest summer toboggan run, part of the **Fun & Action Park**.

Gondolas Fräkmüntegg - Kriens

Gondalas, which became panoramic in 1996, have been serving the line section between Fräkmüntegg and Kriens since 1954. At **Krienseregg**, 1,026 m (3,369 ft), a nature reserve, the **DrachenMoor** (literally, Dragon Moor) features adventure trails and is equipped with five educational platforms reached by catwalks and offering insight into the marsh and moorland habitat, its flora and fauna. Brochures are available and PILU® will be your guide.

Round Trips – Excursions

In summer, take one of the Pilatus round trips, with their multiple gastronomic attractions to tempt the tastebuds.

The Matterhorn; Switzerland's most photographed tourist attraction.

Zermatt

From the outset, in the famous Valais resort of Zermatt, you will only have eyes for the summits: first of all the unmistakable pyramid-shape of the Matterhorn (or Cervin), 4,478 m (14,692 ft) high. The peak was conquered in 1865 by five Englishmen, among them Edward Whymper (1840–1911), led by three local guides; Today climbers arrive en masse to pitch themselves against this magic pyramid.

East of the Matterhorn, in the heart of the Monte Rosa massif, is the Dufourspitze (Pointe Dufour). Culminating at 4,634 m (15,204 ft), it is the second-highest peak in Western Europe after the Mont Blanc. At 4,545 m (14,912 ft), the Dom is the highest summit entirely on Swiss territory and is part of the Mischabel group. The best summit view is from the top of Gornergrat. Despite its modern facilities, which enable it to cater to well over a million visitors a year, the centre of Zermatt has managed to retain the character of a mountain village. Cars are prohibited; all transport is provided by electric vehicles and horse-drawn taxis. The main streets are lined with chic boutiques and classy restaurants, even along the many trails around Zermatt. Take a look at the cemeteries of the English Church, built by the British Alpine Club, and the parish church, near the bridge over the Vispa: some of the mountain climbers who lost their lives attempting to conquer the Matterhorn lie here.

On the other side of the church, the **Matterhorn Museum** traces the history of Zermatt and its famous mountain in an original way.

Excursions from Zermatt

A few minutes' walk behind the station (about 10 minutes) you can take a funicular through a tunnel to the sunny terrace of **Sunnegga** at 2,288 m (7,506 ft), where there's a marmot observation post. To know more about this cute little animal, take the cable car up to **Blauherd**, 2,571 m (8,435 ft) , the start of a Marmot Trail leading back to Sunnegga, lined with wood-carvings depicting its life. There's also an adventure playground at Blauherd, called the Dwarves' Paradise. A panoramic cable car then whisks you up to **Rothorn Paradise**, 3,103 m (10,180 ft).

Between the Matterhorn and Monte Rosa, the Little Matterhorn, 3,884 m (12,743 ft), is a summer skiing domain that can be reached by a cable car which claims to be the highest in Europe. The **Matterhorn Glacier Paradise** has a grotto of ice sculptures, the glacier palace. The new restaurant uses photovoltaic facilities for energy supplies. From here you can tackle the easiest of the 4,000 m mountains; Alpine guides will accompany you to the summit of **Breithorn** (4,164m).

In summer as well as in winter, skiers skim back and forth over the vast slopes of the Theodul glacier/ Plateau Rosa (access by funicular), and across the Italian border. Snowboarders gravitate towards the **Gravity Park**.

Gornergrat-Bahn

Before the Jungfraubahn came into service in 1912, the cogwheel railway of the Gornergrat, 3,089 m (10,135 ft) was the highest, as well as the first of its kind to be electrified. Inaugurated in 1898, the line has been open year round since 1929 and today the rails have doubled to a length of 3,8 km. You get an unbeatable view over the surrounding summits and from the top, a panorama over the Monte Rosa Massif. The silver dome of the **3100 Kulmhotel Gornergrat**, built in 1910 and recently restored, sits over an observatory telescope.

Gornergrat-Bahn: technical data
Type: narrow-gauge electric railway
Taction: cog wheel
Lenght: 9,4 km (5.8 miles)
In service since: 1898
Tunnels: 5
Bridges: 5

Glacier Express

It comes with its wagonload of superlatives: "the world's slowest Express train", "one of the wildest and most fascinating journeys in the history of European railways", "Touch the Sky". These are the slogans used by the railway companies to promote the east-west connection cutting through the Swiss High Alps. Between Zermatt and Sankt Moritz, the Glacier Express runs on the narrow-gauge lines (1000 mm) of the Matterhorn-Gotthard-Bahn (MGB) and the Rhätische Bahn (Rhaetian Railway, RhB). It crosses 291 bridges or viaducts, passes through 91 tunnels and climbs up to the level of the Oberalp Pass at an altitude of 2,033 m (6,670 ft). The trip takes about 8 hours; booking is compulsory for any journey section.

During the summer there are 3 trains daily between Sankt Moritz and Zermatt in both directions; meals are served to you in your seat. One train with a wagon restaurant runs in both directions between Zermatt and Davos. During the winter there is only one daily train from Zermatt to St. Moritz, circulating in each direction.

The Glacier Express was created in 1930, when the directors of the BVZ decided to extend their line from Visp to Brig, joining up the metric-gauge network of the Brig-Visp-Zermatt-Bahn (BVZ), the Furka-Oberalp-Bahn (FO) and the RhB. With the assets of an exclusive saloon car and a reputed winter sports resort at each end of the line–such as Zermatt and Sankt Moritz–the train was an immediate success.

There was, however, one major problem: at the approach of winter, the FO had to take down the contact lines and catenary supports on the Furka Pass stretch and re-install them all again at the beginning of spring. This obstacle was overcome in 1982 with the opening of the long tunnel at the base of the Furka, at the cost of the view over the Rhône glacier. Ever since, the Glacier Express can cross the Swiss Alps all year round. In 2003 the BVZ and FO merged to form the MGB.

If you have the time take the steam train of the Furka summit line (DFB, Dampfbahn Furka Bergstrecke) linking Realp and Oberwald. This is possible from end of June until beginning October, sometimes on week-ends only; it is useful to book seats in advance (pages 49–51).

Mattertal

After leaving Zermatt's new railway station the Glacier Express plunges into a succession of shelters, for the steep-sided Mattertal valley which has always been subject to the whims of nature.

Glacier Wine. The wine village of Visperterminen lies at 1,378 m between Stalden and Visp. Europe's highest-altitude vineyard fills a small space on a slope of 500 m (600 to 1,150). Sun and walled terracing provide a warming chamber ideal for the Heida grape from which the glacier wine is harvested and pressed, the "pearl of Alpine wines". Connoisseurs praise its quality, but also recognized its kick, as it goes straight to the head and legs!

istockphoto.com/Mizar Luca

Between Zermatt and Täsch, shuttle trains provide a link both for travellers arriving by car and for the delivery of merchandise. The train station in Täsch has ultramodern infrastructures in place as well as vast car parks.

The next village, **Randa**, narrowly escaped destruction several times by flooding or falls of serac. Further down the valley, the holiday resort of **Grächen** sits on a sunny balcony overlooking Saint-Nicolas.

Visp (Viège) and Saas Valleys

Level with **Stalden**, the Matter Vispa flows into the Saaser Vispa. Straddling the deep gorge are two bridges, the oldest dating from 1546. Following the branch of the Saas Valley you can reach the well-known holiday resorts of Saas-Grund and Saas-Fee.

After Stalden, the Vispa Valley widens, and the first vineyards appear on the sunny slopes. To the right, you may be able to make out the vineyards of **Visperterminen**, the highest in Europe. Just before **Visp** the cogwheel section of the track ends and the Glacier Express continues on into the Rhône Valley. In the distant past Visp was an important transfer station on the trading routes to

Italy. Today, the town is the site of a chemical plant, one of the main employers of the region. On the northern slope between Visp and Brig, saffron is grown at 1,200m in the mountain village of **Mund**. The saffron museum is housed in the tithe-barn built in 1437.

Brig

As far as Brig, the capital of German-speaking Upper Valais (or Wallis), the train runs parallel to the Simplon line, Paris-Lausanne-Milan. Because of its location at the crossroads of the great mountain passes (Simplon, Furka, Grimsel, Nufenen), Brig has been an important place for trade since the Middle Ages. The town lived its golden age in the 16th

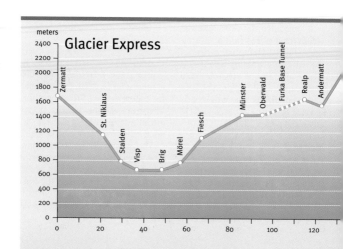

Glacier Express: technical data
Type: narrow-gauge electric railway
Tractions: adhesive + cog wheel
Lenght: 291 km (180.8 miles)
In service since: 1930
Tunnels: 91
Bridges/Viaducs: 291

and 17th centuries under the influence of the merchant family Von Stockalper, and in particular Kaspar Jodok von Stockalper, familiarly known as the King of the Simplon.

Following the modern Bahnhofstrasse, you reach **Sebastiansplatz** and the church of Saint Sebastian dating from 1637. The old Simplon road, lined by majestic patrician mansions, goes from there up to the **Stockalper palace**. The main four-storey building and the lovely arcaded courtyard, with its three massive corner towers topped by gilded domes, were built from 1658 to 1678 under the aegis of the "royal" personage. The complex, which today houses offices, a museum and an art gallery, also includes two other Stockalper mansions.

Official documents confirming the entry of Valais into the Swiss confederation were signed in the first from 16th century, the one belonging to Peter Stockalper.

The second, from the 18th century belonged to Fernanda Stockalper. Above the palace looms the collegial church of the Holy

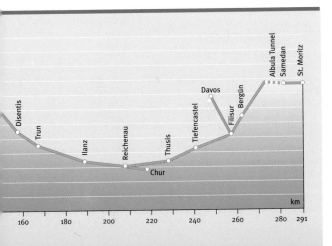

flickr.com/Aletsch Arena

The overwhelming Aletsch Glacier, the longest and largest glacier in Europe.

Spirit from 17th century, and close by is the Ursuline church of the 18th century.

Be sure to visit the big **pilgrim church of Saint Mary's** (Unserer Lieben Frau) in Glis, a village close to Brig which can easily be reached by bus or taxi. The present main building in Renaissance style stands on a Gothic base. The interior is adorned with several superb altars, among them the high altar (1480) and the Supersaxo altar (1519) in the left chapel.

Naters

After leaving Brig station, the Glacier Express runs along the left bank of the Rotten River. There's nothing derogatory about the river's name, it is simply the way the people of the region referred to the Rhône. The train ceased runing through the centre of Naters in 2007. In its historic heart, a 12th-century Romanesque belltower stands next to traditional wood chalets, as well as a charnel house and the Junkernhof (town hall) of the 15th–16th centuries.

Naters is linked to the mountain villages of Blatten and Belalp. This last can be reached by cable car. From the top you get a superb view of the **Aletsch glacier**. At 24 km (14 miles), this is the longest glacier in Europe, with its source in the Jungfrau massif: it was listed by Unesco as a World Heritage site in 2001.

The Aletsch region with its ancient larch and Swiss stone pine woods, shelters the holiday resorts of Riederalp and, further east, Bettmeralp. Together with Fiesch-Eggishorn, they form the **Aletsch Arena** resort region.

Bettmer Alp, Bettmernhorn and Ice-World

A side trip to the Bettmeralp and Bettmerhorn is highly recommended. The shuttle service sweeps you quietly up in just seven minutes from the Betten valley station to the car-free Bettmeralp (1,938 m). A short walk or electric bus-ride takes you to the cable-car which brings you in comfort to the Bettmerhorn (2,647 m). Awaiting you here is a fantastic view over the Great Aletsch Glacier and the Valais and Bernese Alps as well as the Bettmerhorn mountain restaurant with its idiosyncratic, crystalline architecture.

The *Bettmerhorn Ice World* exhibition provides exciting and instructive information about glacier science including the *Aletsch Glacier Fascination* and the historically interesting *Ice Room* multimedia display.

Goms Valley

Carved out thousands of years ago by the Rhône glacier, the valley is self-contained, a country apart. At the valley entrance, the train crosses over a viaduct 31 m (over 10 ft) high and plunges into a helix tunnel from which it emerges at Lax, at the entrance to the Goms Valley.

Located between the important north-south routes of the alpine passes (Nufenen, Furka, Grimsel, Gries and Albrun), settlers arrived in the Bronze Age. The Alamans came into this high valley in the 8th and 9th centuries. They were followed in the 13th and 14th centuries by the Walser from Germany, who gradually replaced the

Glacier Express Technical Information. The Rhaetian Railway (RhB) and Matterhorn-Gotthard Railway (MGB) are private independent companies. Both mountain railways do an excellent job of making valleys accessible. Thanks to the Glacier Express, the RhB and MGB link up to form a truly unique railway experience, with more than 2,000 employees making the unforgettable train journeys a constant success. The Glacier Express product is exploited as a jointly owned brand name. Each company has a 50% share and makes available the same amount of rolling stock, which was completely renewed between 2006 and 2009. All trains today offer panorama coaches both in 1st and 2nd class and are pulled by either RhB or MGB railway engines according to the route they are taking. The RhB engines are exclusively adhesion driven without gearwheel drive, as opposed to MGB which relies on gearwheel driven engines to pull its trains.

Jean-Paul Minder

GLACIER EXPRESS

populations of Romance and Celtic origins. The medieval traditions and culture of that time have been maintained, and the little villages of weatherbeaten brown-black wooden chalets have a timeless charm; half a dozen are listed as part of the Swiss cultural heritage. The wide-spreading Upper Goms Valley is popular with hikers and cross-country skiers.

The main settlement in the Goms Valley is the holiday resort of **Fiesch**. A cable car links it to the lookout point of the **Eggishorn**, 2,827 m (9,603 ft), from where the view carries over the Aletsch glacier and the Alpine summits, stretching from the Jungfrau to the Mont-Blanc.

Ernen, opposite Fiesch, is a lovely village and gateway to the Binntal, renowned for its mineral wealth. Handsomely decorated houses in the centre dating from the 15th to 18th centuries, bear witness to its significant role on the trading route of the great mountain passes.

The church of Saint George has superb baroque altars and an organ dating from 1679; classical recitals are held here during the summer. Niederwald and Reckingen also have fine baroque churches. **Niederwald** is the birthplace of César Ritz, the founder of Ritz and Carlton hotels.

The village of **Münster** has a shrine particularly worthy of interest, attested for the first time in 1309. In **Saint Mary's Church**, admire the finely decorated late-Gothic altar (1509), the rich baroque ornamentation and the Renaissance wooden ceiling.

For the Glory of God. While the valley was booming economically, the artists and artisans of Goms were working for the glory of God, reflected in about 70 richly decorated Baroque church and chapels. To this day, art historians celebrate the altars and sculpted figures which came from the studio of Johann Ritz (1666-1729) and his son Jodok in Seldingen. In the neighbouring village of Reckingen, generations of the Carlen family of organmakers had created their famous instruments since the 17th century; some of them cropping up in foreign lands. And to this day, church-bells ringing in Valais and throughout Switzerland originated from the old Walpen bell-foundry in Reckingen.

Furka Base Tunnel

Just after Oberwald, the last village of the valley to be inhabited year round, the Glacier Express enters the Furka Base Tunnel. It was built from 1973 to 1982 and is 15.4 km (9 miles) long. There is only one metric gauge line, with two crossing points, and it is only used for carrying freight. During the winter the tunnel is the only connection between the Valais and central Switzerland.

Gletsch

The little hamlet of Gletsch has a protected urban landscape of national importance and various sightseeing attractions: the Anglican chapel (built 1908), the exhibition of "the Rhône Glacier landscape over the centuries", small hydroelectric power plants (1899 and 1942), an Alpine cheese dairy, restored meteorological station (1903) and the historic Hotel Glacier du Rhône with its traditionally furnished rooms. The village infopoint will give you more detailed information.

Here the road splits with one branch heading north over the **Grimsel Pass** into the Bernese Oberland, the other going east over the **Furka** into the Gotthard region.

Furka Steam Train

During the summer, the Furka steam train puffs to Realp from Oberwald in the Valais region to Urserental. Admire the pioneering achievements in the middle of magnificent mountain landscape. You will experience an unforgettable journey of surprises through numerous gorges.

In lovingly restored coaches pulled by an over 100-year-old

Dampfbahn Furka-Bergstrecke AG/Beat Moser

The Furka train passes through unique landscapes on its journey.

railway engine, you travel at leisurely speeds over boldly designed bridges, through narrow tunnles and past rock-faces. The train makes one stop in order to collect water. Book your seat in advance.

Furka steam train: technical data
Route length: 17,838 km
Track width: 1000 mm
Maximum inclination:
Adhesive: 35/00
Rack-rail: 118/00
Rack System: Abt

FURKA-STORY

The construction of the cogwheel railway over the Furka Pass was first started in 1911 by the Brig-Furka-Disentis Railway (BFD) and was brought to a halt in 1915 due to the outbreak of World War I, in addition to various financial and technical problems.

After BFD's bankruptcy in 1923, construction resumed one year later by the newly formed Furka-Oberalp Railway (FO) with massive support from the two neighbouring railway companies, the Rhaetian Railway (RhB) and the Visp-Zermatt Railway (VZ) which have since merged to become the Brig-Visp-Zermatt Railway (BVZ).

The route was opened in 1925 and electrified in 1942 with an overhead contact line, but 40 years later (1982) it was closed down. The nationally planned, legally prescribed dismantling was held up by railway enthusiasts, who founded the Furka Railway Club (Verein Furka-Bergstrecke) in 1983. In 1985 the Dampfbahn Furka-Bergstrecke AG (Furka Cogwheel Steam Railway Company) was selected to run the club.

Extensive renovations on the old mountain railway began in Realp. The overhead contact line, still in place, was dismantled. Financing of these operations was made possible mainly

flickr.com/Wichary

Gleis 1

Dampfzug

Muttbach-Belvédère

Realp

through donations and the highly successful sale of shares to railway buffs.

The first units of rolling stock were acquired from various Swiss narrow-gauge railways and restored. The Realp-Tiefenbach stretch was operational and open to the public in 1992 and extended to the Furka Summit Tunnel just one year later.

It took eight years for the excavation of the tunnel and other works to be completed before the train could ride the full stretch to Gletsch. On August 12, 2010, the last stretch between Gletsch and Oberwald was opened. The railway company possesses a Swiss federal concession and therefore comes under the supervision of the Federal Transportation Office (BAV). Operations, maintenance and rolling stock, as well as the accompanying relations with the public are, however, exclusively guaranteed by volunteers. Over 8,000 members of this railway buffs' club (Förderverein, FVB) from all over Europe make their services available for free. Of its 23 sections, twelve are in Switzerland, nine in Germany and one each in Belgium and the Netherlands.

Four of originally ten HG 3/4 steam engines built between 1912 and 1913 in Winterthur were sold to Vietnam by the Furka-Oberalp-Bahn (FO) after the electrification of the railway in 1947. From the 1970's, they stood around idle in the south of Vietnam until members of the association tracked them down. Under a "Back to Switzerland" motto, two engines that were still intact along with functional spare parts from the two others, were brought back from Vietnam at great expense and effort.

Two HG 4/4 steam engines delivered directly to Vietnam by the Swiss Locomotive and Machine Factory (SLM) were also acquired and brought back. By 1993, after thorough restoration in the Meiningen steam-engine works (BRD), two of the HG 3/4 engines were already good and fit for service.

The *Furkahorn* HG 3/4 carries its original factory number 1, the *Gletschhorn* HG 3/4 number 9. Taken over by the Matterhorn-Gotthard Railway and comprehensively renovated, the original FO engine HG 3/4, number 4, has been back in service on the mountain route since July 2006.

Weisshorn HG 2/3 number 6, the steam engine operating since 1902 on the Visp-Zermatt Railway, transferred in 1989 to the DFB and since then it has provided sterling service at the head of the old-fashioned trains chugging past the Rhône Glacier.

Urseren Valley

This alpine valley, a west-east link between the Furka and Oberalp passes, became a strategic crossroads during the 13th century. The wild gorges of the Schöllenen were made practicable at the end of the 12th century, thus creating the quickest north-south route through the Alps from the Vierwaldstättersee through the Reuss Valley, the Schöllenen Gorges and Urseren Valley, finally reaching northern Italy via the Saint Gotthard Pass and the Leventina Valley.

The train line follows the Reuss river, soon arriving into **Hospental**, where a branch of the line leaves for the Saint-Gotthard Pass. A fortified tower dating from around 1200 was the home of the lords of Hospental. The parish church has a handsome altar carved by Jodok Ritz.

Andermatt, with its late-Romanesque church from the 13th-century currently resembles a huge building site as construction works are currently underway, financed by an Egyptian investor. However, for an unbeatable view over the whole region, take the cable car from Andermatt to **Gemsstock**, at 2,961 m (9,715 ft).

Oberalp Pass

After its halt at Andermatt the train moves back onto the rack line and begins a series of wide curves that take it up to 2,033 m (6,670 ft). At the top of the pass is the **Oberalp Lake**. This is the departure point for superb hikes, one of the best being to the idyllic setting of **Toma Lake**, the source of the Rhine. The train then starts its descent, passing through a series of anti-avalanche galleries.

Anterior Rhine Valley

You are now in the Graubünden (Grischun or Grisons) canton, one of the areas of Switzerland where the ancient language of Romansh is still spoken. Green meadows, forests, dark rocky peaks draped with snow, this is the Anterior Rhine Valley, known in Romansh as Surselva ("above the forest"). Today **Surselva** is an appreciated holiday region that has not yet been overwhelmed by tourism. Once over the pass, you enter the commune of **Tujetsch**, which spreads over several villages, the most important of which is **Sedrun**.

The 17th-century Saint Vigil church has a Romanesque bell-tower dating back to the 13th century; the interior contains several carved and baroque altars.

Disentis (**Mustér** in Romansh) stands on the site of a monastery founded by Saint Sigisbert in the 8th century. The Benedictine abbey enjoyed a golden age during the 10th to 11th centuries

IMPORTANT WATERWAYS

Throughout your journey on the Glacier Express, you will have been struck by the many waterways, going in different directions, that have accompanied you along the way. The rivers have scooped out star-shaped valleys from the core of the Alps. They form one watershed running from north to south and another running east to west. Being the source of both a reservoir of drinking water and of natural energy provided through hydraulic power, the significance of these important springs, along with several rivers, extends far beyond the Swiss borders.

From Brig to Oberwald, the still narrow stream of the Rhône burbles along in the opposite direction to the train – it is headed for the Mediterranean.

Near the Nufenen Pass is the source of the Ticino river which joins the Po and flows into the Adriatic just south of Venice. The Aar river rises above Gletsch in the Grimsel region. Heading north, it crosses the canton of Bern before joining the Reuss River further downstream along the Aargau; together they combine with the Rhine and flow towards the North Sea.

The Furka Reuss rises at the Furka Pass, the Gotthard Reuss rises in the Gotthard mountain range and they thunder together into the Schöllenen gorge in the direction of the Vierwaldstätter See and Lucerne.

The Vorderrhein (Anterior Rhine) rises near the Lake Toma at the Oberalp Pass, joining the Hinterrhein (Posterior Rhine) on its way past Reichenau. Like the Rhine, it flows 1,320 km further into the North Sea. Just before St Moritz, you will cross the Inn. The river rises in the Maloja region and meets the Danube at Passau in Germany, ending in Romania and flowing into the Black Sea.

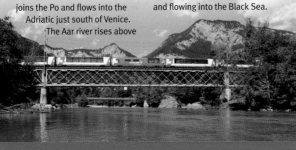

under the Othon emperors, who were interested in the passage south via the Lukmanier Pass. The abbey is still a training centre today. Even though the Convent Church of Saint Martin was plundered by French troops in 1799, several altars of great value were preserved, including the Castelberg altar of 1572. The convent museum reveals more about the abbey's history.

The train stops for quite a long time in Disentis, the engine is changed here before continuing along the Rhätische Bahn.

Sedrun and Porta Alpina. Particularly imposing are the two vertical shafts reaching down from Sedrun to a depth of 800 m into the construction site of the Gotthard Base Tunnel. They serve to remove material but also to facilitate technical safety in addition to any improvements in the construction work. *Porta Alpina* is the canton of Graubünden's futuristic project to provide the base tunnel with a subterranean railway station at Sedrun. It also involves using the existing shafts as lifts. The project remains a dream for the time being, although the safety of the tunnel certainly speaks in its favour and access to Graubünden, presently separated, could be significantly shortened.

Trun is considered to be the cradle of the Graubünden canton. The Grey League (Grauer Bund), was founded at the foot of a maple tree, on the spot where the Chapel of Saint Anne, with its grand courtyard, stands today. The Sursilvan Regional Museum, in the former convent cloister, unveals more local history.

Ilanz

Founded by the Celts in 765, this market town received its city charter at the end of the 13th century. Ilanz is considered to be the "first town on the Rhine". Strolling around the old centre with its winding, narrow streets, you will discover some fine patrician mansions of the 17th and 18th centuries. Remains of the old fortress are still standing — such as the red tower and the 16th-century upper tower. The late-Gothic parish church has a belltower that served for defensive purposes. The **Surselva Regional Folklore Museum** is set up in the Casa Carniec.

After Ilanz, the train plunges into what people here like to call Switzerland's Grand Canyon, the wild and romantic deep **Gorges of the Rhine** which were created by an immense rockslide.

Reichenau

At Reichenau, with its 17th-century castle, the Anterior and Posterior Rhines meet, and the Bernina Express (Chur-Sankt Moritz-Tirano) joins the Glacier Express.

Domleschg and Albula Valley

As far as Thusis, the Posterior Rhine Valley is called the Domleschg. It forms a corridor leading on to the most important Graubünden passes, a position that made this valley much sought after in centuries past. Witness to this are the numerous fortresses and castles clinging to the slopes and crowning peaks.

The imposing castle of **Rhäzüns**, reputed for its mineral water, was mentioned for the first time in the 13th century. Saint Peter's parish church is adorned with Gothic murals, probably the work of the same anonymous artist who painted the marvellous frescoes in Saint George's Church, just outside Rhäzüns.

On the way to Thusis, the vestiges of old **feudal mansions** can be seen on both sides of the track: Niederjuvalta and Oberjuvalta, the handsome castle of Ortenstein, the ruins of Alt Sin and Neu Sin, Rietberg Castle and the ruins of Hasensprung. **Thusis** itself is dominated by the fortress of the Hohenrätien, which probably dates back to the 11th century. Just before you reach the high hill where the castle stands, at the moment when the train crosses the Posterior Rhine flowing down

Rhätische Bahn, Chur/A. Badrutt

The Landwasser Viaduct, a technical masterpiece, built in 1902.

from the San Bernardino, you get a glimpse of the wild gorges of the Via Mala, made famous in 1934 by Swiss writer John Knittel's novel of the same name.

The 122 km of railway engineer's art comprising the Albula and Bernina lines has been UNESCO listed since July 2008.

The Glacier Express follows the Albula River, passing the ruins of Campi, riding over the narrow gorge of Schyn and crossing the viaduct of Solis, 89 m (292 ft) high, to reach the junction of **Tiefencastel**. The little town on the road to the Julier Pass has a beautiful baroque parish church. **Saint Peter in Mistail**, a few kilometres further on, is better known; this large 8th-century Carolingian church is one of the oldest and nicest in Switzerland.

Viaduct over the Landwasser

After the localities of Surava and Alvaneu, look out for one of the world's greatest feats of railway engineering: the elegant stone viaduct straddling the Landwasser, 130 m (439 ft) long and 65 m (213 ft) high. It forms a huge arc with a curve radius of 100 m (328 ft), and plunges directly into a tunnel in the almost vertical cliffside. This is an architectural masterpiece, if you consider that it was built in 1902.

Albula Line

Filisur, at the beginning of the Albula line, is a charming old village with houses decorated in typical Engadine style. Thanks to the railway branch line that departs from here to go to Davos, it is also an important junction for the Rhaetian Railway. The train has to climb 700 m (2,296 ft) in the 12-km (8-mile) stretch between Filisur and Preda — no mean challenge for the railway engineers. The brilliant way they solved the problem counts among the greatest achievements of the early 20th century. After winding through the first helix tunnel, the train climbs to the holiday village of **Bergün**.

It is here, right next to the station, that the **Albula Railway Museum** opened in June 2012, an attraction for families and railway enthusiasts. Various original objects are on show, such as the world's last "Crocodile locomotive". The museum provides a

Bergün/Bravuogn
1372 m

Chur

ALVANEU

historical and current view of Switzerland's most spectacular railway, which is part of UNESCO's heritage.

Then begins the remarkable stretch that forms a veritable "train ladder", meandering back and forth, round and about, the rail passes through five helix tunnels, two standard tunnels, nine viaducts and two galleries before finally arriving at the little village of Preda. ving at the little village of Preda. Those who want to admire this technical marvel in close-up can walk down to Bergün by the marked footpath, illustrated with panels explaining the history of the line. In winter, the road between Preda and Bergün is transformed into a popular sledging track.

The Albula tunnel starts at **Preda**. Built from 1898 to 1902, it is 5.8 km (3.6 miles) long, and with a maximum altitude of 1,820 m (5,971 ft), is the highest transalpine tunnel in Europe.

Engadine

The train exits the Albula tunnel in the Val Bever, a narrow side valley of the Engadine. With its pleasant landscape, transparent lakes, mild climate and incomparable light, the Engadine is one of the most beautiful regions in Switzerland. The villages are also very attractive, their elegant houses embellished with sgraffito

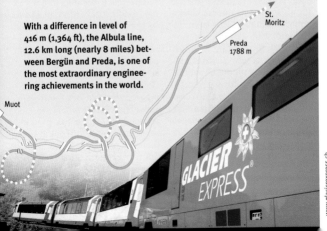

With a difference in level of 416 m (1,364 ft), the Albula line, 12.6 km long (nearly 8 miles) between Bergün and Preda, is one of the most extraordinary engineering achievements in the world.

Muot

St. Moritz

Preda
1788 m

www.glacierexpress.ch

Houses typical to the village of Madulain in Engadin, characterised by their Sgraffito design.

designs. Year round there is something to please nature and sports fans.

Samedan, the capital of High Engadine, has an unusual claim to fame: the highest aerodrome in Europe. Several beautiful Engadine houses in the well-preserved village date from the 16th to 18th centuries. One of them, Chesa Planta, contains a museum of 18th and 19th-century interior decoration, the cultural archives of the region and a Romansh library; lessons in that charming old language are also given (it sounds something like a mixture of French, German, Italian and Latin). St Peter's funerary chapel dates from the 15th century, but the original building was already acknowledged in 1139.

Celerina is the sunniest spot in the whole Engadine and is the gateway to a marvellous skiing domain; it also makes a good base for hikers. The cable car takes you to the hiking and skiing region of Marguns. Every August, Celerina stages a jazz festival. Beyond the bridge over the Inn river a little outside of town, the San Gian Church sits on *Via San Gian*. It has one Romanesque and one larger Gothic tower whose pointed crown fell victim to lightning at the end of the 17th century. Inside, be sure to see the ornately carved wooden ceiling and the frescoes from the 15th century in the choir stalls. From here it isn't far to the valley station of Muottas Mragl.

Celerina-Cresta is the end of the world famous Sankt Moritz bobsleigh course, the '**Cresta Run**'.

St. Moritz

The place became famous in the Middle Ages (1466) thanks to its hot springs, already exploited in pre-Roman times. It is hard to imagine that in 1830 only 200 people lived in Sankt Moritz!

In the 19th century, Johannes Badrutt founded the Kulm by taking over the lease of a family pension. His establishment was the cornerstone of the luxury hotel scene in Sankt Moritz, and since then the town has continued to flourish, never looking back. The prestigious Kulm was run by Badrutt's descendants until the end of the 20th century when it was taken over.

The perfect harmony of landscape and sunshine contribute to the charm of Sankt Moritz and impressive spa centres, cultural interests and the National Park all add to its popularity and world famed atmosphere.

Among the few historic sights in the village, look for the leaning tower, remains of the long-disappeared pilgrimage church of Saint Maurice. Sankt Moritz-Bad is the site of the impressive spa.

The splendid **Carlton Hotel** was built as a private residence for the Tsar Nicholas II, but the October Revolution in 1917 prevented him from ever staying there.

The **Engadine Museum**, located on Via del Bagn 39, is worth a visit. It displays various traditional art and handicraft collections. The neighbouring **Segantini Museum** is devoted to the famous Italian painter Giovanni Segantini (1858–99) who spent the last years of his life in the Engadine. His works portray life in the region in the 19th century.

Sankt Moritz has facilities for every sport imaginable: the Winter Olympics have been held here twice (1928 and 1948). A spectacular annual sports event is held in Sankt Moritz in March: the **Engadine Ski Marathon** sees as many as 13,000 participants gliding over the frozen lake. The funicular takes you from the village to to Corviglia (2,486 m) and from there a cable car climbs up to the Piz Nair. The "Signalbahn" from the St Moritz spa also takes you up to the Corviglia area.

Traction Power. Traction power is a special current with its own frequency (16 2/3 Hz). The Swiss Federal Railways (SFR) produce 75% of it from their own hydroelectric plants. The SFR distribute the necessary power for running their trains using a nationwide low voltage network. In addition to its own production, the SFR buys power from the "normal network". This power, with a frequency of 50 Hz, must first be converted to "traction power" with a three-times lower frequency before it can be fed into the contact lines. This transformed power represents a quarter of the SFR traction power. Besides the four machine groups, two single-phase groups have been installed in the Sils power station. These produce power exclusively for the Rhaetian Railway (RhB), which feeds its contact line network, just like the SFR, single-phase rather than triple-phase power with a frequency of 16 2/3 rather than 50 Hz. With the two traction power generators, 45% of the whole traction power needs of the Rhaetian Railway are covered.

Davos

Davos has bee well known for its curative mountain air and for its choice of winter sports since the 19th century.

Chur and Davos

Chur, the departure point of the Bernina Express line is the administrative capital of the Graubünden; some of the trains also leave from Davos.

Chur

Chur is one of the oldest towns in Switzerland, settled in Neolithic times. It was also the capital of the Roman province of Rhaetia before becoming a bishopric in the 5th century.

The charming old town, hidden away behind more modern districts, is dominated by the 18th-century baroque **Episcopal Palace** and the 12th–13th-century **St Maria Himmelfahrt** (Cathedral of the Assumption). The interior of the Romanesque-Gothic shrine is adorned with several beautiful statues and a splendid late-Gothic triptych.

In the **adjacent museum**, you can admire the richly endowed cathedral treasury. The canons' houses, defensive towers, a theological seminary, the old convent church of St Lucius—and a vineyard—all belong to the bishopric.

Down below the castle, look in at the **Rätische Museum**, housed in a patrician mansion next to St Martin's Church. It displays several interesting collections on the history of the canton, following from its origins through to the 20th century.

Narrow winding streets lead to the Kornplatz, a square dominated by the Town Hall (15th–16th centuries), then to the Postplatz, in the town centre. The Cantonal **Museum of Fine Arts** lies to the northeast, in the Villa Planta. There you can see works by Alberto Giacometti and the Giacometti family, Angelika Kauffmann, Giovanni Segantini and Ernst Ludwig Kirchner.

Continuing northwards, you reach the Cantonal **Museum of Nature** (*Bünder Naturmuseum*) devoted to natural science and also to the environmental education and the use of resources.

Next door is a **Wine Museum** (Weinbaumuseum); book ahead. Wine has been produced in the Herrschaft, the sunny right-hand slope of the Graubünden part of

---

Albula Adventure Train. The brown cult-engine of the RhB draws families and railway buffs to the lovely Albula Valley. Their goal is the Albula Railway Museum where, over an area of 1,300 sq m, more than 400 exhibits cover 100 years of railway history. The route takes you from Preda to Bergün, unvealing the secrets of this UNESCO site along the way . On Sundays you can experience the old -fashioned wooden open-air viewing carriages which form part of the RhB's railway paradise.

the Rhine Valley, ever since the 17th century, and Herrschäftler wines, such as Maienfelder, Malanser and Fläscher have a good reputation.

istockphoto.com/Bouwman

Journeys in the Driver's Seat. This is the dream of every railway buff. Accompanied by a professional railwayman, you take the driver's place in an RhB engine for a journey through the Albula Valley or over the highest railway transversal in the Alps, along the Bernina line. The train curves its way through craggy valleys and over admirable railway constructions and you are right at the heart of it! You will feel as powerful as a magician at the head of a train which, in spite of its huge tonnage, climbs the mountain heights with ease. Explore the Unesco World Heritage Site in an exceptional manner—diploma and snapshots included. For further information, go to www.rhb.ch, or visit the stations of the Rhaetian Railway or telephone the Rail Service: +41 81 288 65 65.

Bernina Express

The Rhaetian Railway (RhB), is not only the official company of the Graubünden canton, but also the biggest and most important.

At the end of the 19th century, attempting to find a way to the south, the RhB created an extraordinary transalpine line, the Bernina. It became a Unesco World Heritage site in 2008. Leaving the green valleys of the Graubünden, the train climbs up to the glaciers and pass of the Bernina, tackling a 7% gradient without the help of cogwheels. On this stretch it's hard to decide what is the most impressive: the grandiose landscape or the technical prowess. The contrast between the eternal snows of the Graubünden Alps and the Mediterranean charm of Val Poschiavo and the Valtellina is particularly striking.

In 1949 the RhB received the go-ahead to exploit the short stretch between the Swiss frontier and Tirano in the Italian Piedmont, and to set up their southern terminus in this town. This enabled the creation of the Bernina Express. Today, the panoramic cars serving this line give the passengers a unique and memorable experience.

Varying Routes

The Bernina Express follows the same route as the Glacier Express from Reichenau to Sankt Moritz;

you will find the description of this stretch on p. 42–59.

Depending on the season, the timetable, and the final destination, the train starts in Davos and then a connection is available in Filisur or, on exception, it stops in Sankt Moritz (see p.56-57). Let's start from Davos.

Davos

The town of *Tavaus* or *Dafaas* is first mentioned in the Chur archives in 1160. In the 13th century, the lords from the northern Walser valleys (Austria) settled here and guaranteed autonomy for the new Walser village. At the beginning of the 16th century, the people converted to the Protestant Reformation. It was in the mid-19th century that Alexander Spengler discovered the medicinal benefits of high-altitude air for lung ailments. This resulted in the quick development of Davos along with its larch forest and picturesque lake.

Today, **Davos Dorf** and **Davos Platz** form the highest town in Europe (1560 m) with more than 12,000 inhabitants. The town nestles with other villages like Weisen, Frauenkirch, Glaris et Monstein in the Landwasser Valley, surrounded by mountain ranges soaring to heights of 2,000 to 3,000 metres. Needless to say, lovers of sports will find everything they need here. **Parsenn**, **Rinerhorn**, **Schatzalp/Strela Pischa** and **Jakobshorn** offer vast stretches of winter ski pistes and in summer a large quantity of trails and biking routes.

On the top of the Weissfluh (at Parsenn 2834 m (9,888 ft)), is the federal institute's centre for the study of snow and avalanche research—the only one in the world—and it retains over 70 years worth of information concerning daily measurements.

Thomas Mann wrote of Davos in his novel 'The Magic Mountain' (1924), while his wife was undergoing treatment in a sanatorium. Do not miss the futuristic **Kirchner Museum** (1992); it houses a collection of works by the famous German Expressionist painter Ernst Ludwig Kirchner, who lived in Davos from 1918 until his death in 1938.

The cream of economy and politics gather here in Davos every year for the **World Economy Forum** (**WEF**). Less sophisticated, but nevertheless world famous, is the **Spengler Cup**. This international ice hockey tournament was first

---

Bernina Express Technical data:
Type: narrow-gauge electric railway
Traction: adhesive
Length: 144 km (89.5 miles)
In service since: 1973
Tunnels/galleries: 55
Bridges/viaducts: 196

organised in 1923 by Carl Spenger (son of Alexander Spengler) and is staged here annually in December.

Landwassertal

The Landwasser Valley continues between Davos and Filisur. Over bridges and through tunnels, the train traverses the **Zugenschlucht**. From the Bärentritt look-out above the gorges, the view encompasses 360°.

After Wiesen, the train crosses the longest bridge of the RhB network: the **Wiesner viaduct**, 204 m (689 ft) long and 89 m (289 ft) high. It ends just before Filisur. From here the train continues on, following the Albula Valley (pages 56-67).

Muottas Muragi

After crossing the flat lowlands of Samerdan and before arriving in Pontresina you reach the valley station of **Muottas Muragi**. This peak culminates at an altitude of 2,456 m (8,058 ft) and is considered the most fabulous look-out point in the High Engadine. It is reached via a funicular that has to negotiate a 54% gradient. From the top, the view takes in the entire majestic and breathtaking mountain landscape. You can choose to either follow the path which is lined with signs explaining the local climate, or go hiking on the Oberen Schafberg, site of the painter Giovanni Segantini, to the lovely alpine pastures of Languard.

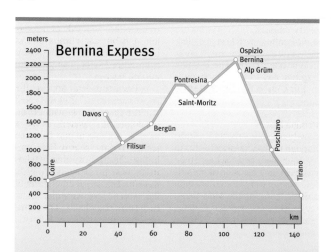

Pontresina

One of the principal holiday resorts of the Graubünden, Pontresina is proudly situated on a protected terrace, surrounded by high summits. A wide variety of activities and entertainment are on offer here during both the summer and winter months.

High above the town, see the five-sided **Spaniards' Tower**, dating from the 12th century, the baroque parish church and Romanesque **Saint Mary's Church**, its interior decorated with 12th-and 15th-century frescoes. In the town centre, the **Alpine Museum** in the Mountain-Climbing School headquarters illustrates all the facets of this sport.

Take a romantic trip in a horse-drawn carriage to discover the diverse local flora in the very pretty **Val Roseg**.

At Pontresina station, the electric current changes from alternate to continuous. The Bernina Express has to change engines and link up to two other electric cars.

Bernina Massif

Slowly but surely the train climbs through the sparse larch forests to the high **Morteratsch plateau**, then passes to the other side of the valley, where it continues to gain altitude thanks to the Montebello curve. The view over the spectacular Bernina massif is ever more impressive. Numerous peaks surround the sparkling **Morteratsch Glacier**: Piz Paul, 3,905 m (12,812 ft); Bellavista, 3,827 m (12,556 ft); Piz Bernina—at 4,049 m (13,285 ft) the highest of the Graubünden peaks; Piz Morteratsch, 3,751 m (12,307); and Piz Boval, 3,353 m (11,001 ft). By the time the train reaches the Bernina Suot station (also called Bernina Häuser), it has passed the tree line and entered a landscape of scrubby meadows and alpine moorland.

The next stop is **Bernina Diavolezza**, the station for the Diavolezza cable car. The "Devil's Mountain", 2,973 m (3,754 ft), part of the Bernina massif, is one of Switzerland's biggest skiing domains. Skiers can practise their skills on the glacier up until summer. On the other side of the valley, a cable car climbs to Piz Lagalb, 2,959 m (9,708 ft) where experienced skiers can go down into **Val Poschiavo**.

A few bends later appears the **Lago Bianco** dam, 2,284 m (7,493 ft). The lake gets its name from the colour of its waters, as white as milk, coming in part from the icefields of the nearby Piz Cambrena. The railway line reaches its highest point at the *Ospizio Bernina* station, at an altitude of 2,253 m (7,392 ft) without any help from cogwheels. The Bernina Pass also marks a linguistic

Observation coaches on the Bernina pass, close to the Alp Grüm.

Rhätische Bahn, Chur/A. Badrutt

you can see the mirror-like waters of the Lago di Poschiavo down in the valley; on clear days the view reaches as far as the Valtellina and the Orobi Alps. After the little Palü Lake near Cavaglia, an old staging post, more bends take the train into the Val Poschiavo. Between here and Tirino the train descends another 600 m.

Val Poschiavo

Before 1913, when the Bernina Line used to close down for the winter, this valley was isolated from the rest of Switzerland for months on end. So it's hardly surprising, that the population of the 34-km (21-mile) valley should turn towards its Italian neighbour, the Valtellina. The people had in common their language and traditions; the villages have a definite Mediterranean character.

The farmers cultivate buckwheat, used to make *pizzoccheri*, a local speciality consisting of wholewheat noodles cooked with potatoes and cabbage and served with cheese.

Passing the tiny villages of Cadra and San Carlo, the train arrives at **Poschiavo**, the main town. If the narrow streets and **palazzi** seem unusually clean and bright, it's because it has been entirely renovated in recent years. In 1987, an avalanche of rocks and mud partially devastated the town. It was rebuilt, thanks to

frontier: if you continue into neighbouring Val Poschiavo, Italian is spoken.

Alp Grüm

At Ospizio Bernina the road and railway separate, the road climbing to a pass at 2,323 m (7,621 ft), the train embarking on a superb panoramic stretch beyond Alp Grüm, 2,091 m (6,860 ft). From there, you could almost reach out and touch the **Palü Glacier** filling the valley between the eastern point of the Palü, 3,998 m (13,117 ft) and the Piz Varuna, 3,453 m (11,329 ft). On the bare rock you can clearly see the traces left by the glacier thousands of years ago, when it was higher.

From Alp Grüm to Poschiavo, the train has to descend 1,100 m (3,281 ft) over a distance of 5 km (3 miles) as the crow flies. This is achieved by an impressive series of bends. From the highest curve, funds collected in an nationwide campaign of solidarity.

In the centre stands the **Town Hall** and its tower, originally a 12th-century dwelling. Opposite, you see the 15th–16th-century convent **Church of San Vittore** with its fine Romanesque belltower. Don't miss the baroque church, a little further south, and its dome dating from the beginning of the 18th century.

The most majestic patrician mansions are in the "Spanish" districts. They were built in the 19th century by émigrés, mostly confectionery-makers, who had made their fortunes in Spain and elsewhere and returned home to spend it. Housed in the typical Palazzo De Bassus-Mengotti e Casa Tomé, the **Museo Poschiavino** documents the valley's history.

Medicinal Herbs and Glacier Garden. Some 25 years ago, an association was founded in Val Poschiavo to promote the cultivation and production of medicinal herbs in the valley. On the basis of its topography and the climatic conditions, the valley is ideal for this kind of cultivation. The region combines the alpine climate of the upper valley with the almost Mediterranean climate of the lower valley to generate a particularly large variety of herbs. Organic herbs are much sought after on the Swiss market. They include yarrow, lady's mantel, thyme, buckhorn plantain, nettle, mallow and melissa. Using them in the making of tea brings out their aroma and fragrance. This niche product is today attracting more and more customers and providing the people of Poschiavo with an attractive alternative to traditional farming.

The Glacier Garden is located about 500m south of the Cavaglia railway station and is easily accessible by following the signposted path. The "Giants' Pots" form an extraordinary natural phenomenon. Over the course of thousands of years, tumbling around with the powerful perpetually swirling currents of prehistoric glacier water, the boulders have been ground by the so-called glacier mills into the rock-faces to hollow out smooth caverns and breaches (entrance free from June to October, guided group tour by appointment).

Tradition. Weaving is one of mankind's oldest handicrafts. Clothes, underwear, household goods, carpets and much, much more were all woven. Their development reflects technical progress and has left its mark on economic history, often in a tragic manner. Today, textiles are manufactured for the most part industrially and the handicraft has largely disappeared. Not so in Poschiavo. There you will still find hand-operated looms. The professional weavers, all women, operate at the cutting edge between handicraft and art, and between tradition and modern design. Using such authentic materials as linen, wool, cotton and silk, they create products that, both simple and precious, beautify daily life and will last for years to come.

After Poschiavo, an unusual experience awaits passengers as the train travels through the middle of the picturesque villages of San Antonio and Le Prese—but along the main road and amongst the traffic! At an altitide of 965 m, both Le Prese and the village of Miralago are pleasant summer holiday resorts on the shores of the Lago di Poschiavo.

Brusio Circular Viaduct

After Miralago, on the south shore, the valley rises steeply. The railway follows two wide curves at **Brusio** before making a triumphant entrance at Brusio station over one the most spectacular works of railway engineering in existence: a **curving**, **sloping viaduct** 116 m (351 ft) long, making a complete circular turn of 360°. Normally this sort of technical solution was only used in helix tunnels. In the middle of the loop you can pause to admire three sculptures by artist Cristiano Paganini.

The train passes through chestnut tree forests, vineyards and tobacco fields. The wine here is Swiss produced although the product will be similar to the Italian vine of Valtellina; you can try it in Tirano. The train reaches the Swiss frontier at **Campocologno**, which it crosses without stopping. The customs officials will be waiting at Tirano.

Tirano

Several times in the past, Tirano, along with the entire Valtellina, was a vassal of the Graubünden. Hoping to control all the roads through the Alps, rulers from all the powerful nations in Europe disputed this fertile valley, stretching from the Stilfserjoch in Lombardy to Lake Como. The last foreign occupiers of the Valtellina were the Austrians, before it was incorporated into the newly unified Italy in 1860.

Situated at the crossroads of numerous transport pathways, Tirano, in the province of Sondrio (Lombardy), is a small, pretty and typically Italian city, its squares lined with restaurants, shops and outdoor cafés. The main building, the **pilgrim church of the Madonna of Tirano**, was consecrated in 1533. The shrine, in Renaissance style, was one of the most important religious sites of the Valtellina. When the Bernina Express crosses its forecourt, traffic stops to grant the red train priority.

The terminal station of the RhB is on the right bank of the river Adda, which flows through town, alongside the *Stazione Ferrovie dello Stato* which has connections for Italy. You are now well south of the Alps. During the summer, you can take one of the Bernina Express buses to Lugano in Switzerland, a departure point for other rail discoveries.

A masterpiece of construction; the circular viaduct from Brusio.

Vereina Line

Landquart is in the Graubünden Herrschaft, where Johanna Spyri (1827–1901) set her novels about Heidi, the Swiss girl who lived in her grandfather's chalet in **Maienfeld**. The tourist industry often refers to the area as **Heidiland**.

Departing from Landquart, a train follows the Vereina Line to Klosters and on through the Vereina Tunnel to Sagliains and Scuol (Schuls) in the Lower Engadine. For the return trip, climb aboard the train for Sankt Moritz which crosses the Engadine valley you could travel through the Engadine Valley to Sankt Moritz, passing alongside the magnificent **Swiss National Park**.

Prättigau

After allowing yourself a final glance over the vineyards of the Herrschaft, the train crosses a narrow transverse valley that separates it from the Prättigau. In the

14th century, the Walser settled in this long valley, the northernmost of all those in the Graubünden, at the frontier with the Austrian Vorarlberg. The wooden houses, and the German dialect spoken by the population, are typical of the Walser. To the north stands the Rhätikon massif formed of Dolomitic rock; its highest summit is the Schesaplan, culminating at 2,967 m (9,735 ft), which is popular with mountain climbers.

Grüsch boasts several handsome patrician houses and a late-Gothic church. At **Jenaz**, a stone circle shows that the Prättigau valley was known to the Celts. All good skiers are familiar with the name of **Küblis**, as it is the arrival post of the Parsenn descent. Don't miss the stained-glass windows (1921) by Augusto Giacometti in the late-Gothic **church of Saint Nicholas**; in the chancel you can see 15th-century mural paintings. **Serneus** is renowned for its hot sulphur springs.

Klosters

Before the British royal family popped up here, it was the site of a Premonstratensian convent, founded in the 13th century but abandoned after the Reformation. When the road and railway line were built in the 19th century, tourism began to take off.

The present resort of Klosters, with its grand hotels, chic boutiques, summer concerts and widespread facilities for sporting and leisure activities, does everything to provide entertainment worthy of its wealthy and distinguished guests.

Inside the 13th-century **Abbey Church** that sits in the town centre, you can admire a series of Gothic murals as well as three stained-glass windows designed by Augusto Giacometti, dating from 1928. There's an interesting **folklore museum** (Heimatmuseum) in the 16th-century farm quaintly called the Nutlihüschi.

A cable car from Klosters-Dorf takes you to Madrisa Saaseralp and its adventure trail. The cable car of the **Gotschnagrat**, at an altitude of 2,285 m (7,497 ft), leaves from beside the station from Klosters-Platz and also ensures a link with the huge skiing and hiking domain of **Parsenn** above Davos. The **Silvretta region**, on the Austrian border east of Klosters, mostly attracts hikers.

If heading for Davos the line crosses the Landquart River over a modern bridge and begins the climb to the Wolfgang Pass, through two helix tunnels.

Vereina Tunnel

Opened in 1999, the Vereina Tunnel, 19.1 km (almost 12 miles) long, connects the Prättigau with the Sankt Moritz-Scuol line, joining it at Sagliains.

At Klosters, the train branches off after the double-track bridge over the Landquart River and soon afterwards enters the Zugwald tunnel, leading to the car-loading station at Selfranga. It then enters the Vereina Tunnel, which rises with a gradient of 1.48% to culminate at 1,463 m (4,799 ft) then descends gently towards Sagliains. The line is predominantly single-track.

Scuol

As you approach Scuol, cradled between the Silvretta mountains and the Engadine Dolomites, you'll see the impressive outline of medieval Tarasp Castle perched on a hilltop. Scuol is the capital of the Lower Engadine, mainly known for its thermal baths and also as the region's terminus for the Rhaetian Railway. The main language used is Rhaeto-Romansh, but German is also spoken.

The town lies in the middle of the Lower Engadine "window", a geologically significant erosion gap in the otherwise gas-tight layer of gneiss and granite. In the area of the "window", gases can force their way upwards from inside the earth through fissures and soft schist, mixing with the groundwater. In this way **mineral springs** are formed and used in spas around Scuol as medicinal springs. From many wells in and around Scuol, mineral drinking water gushes out: alkaline Glauber-salt or magnesium sulphate (Epsom salts) and ferrate, whose digestive properties were already known to the ancient Romans. These springs include Europe's richest source of **Glauber-salt** water, bearing the name "Lucius" with a total mineral content of over 17g per litre. Many of these mineral springs contain natural carbon dioxide.

Other sites worth visiting include the **Lower Engadine Museum**, the late Gothic **St George's church** (1516) and the beautiful houses, their façades covered in sgraffito paintings, which surround the fountains on two squares. Among the historic houses in the upper village, Scuol Sora, is the old parsonage. The Gurlainer Bridge over the Inn river can be classed as a technological triumph.

Above Scuol is **Motta Naluns**, the starting point for walkers, mountain bikers and para-gliders. On the right side of the valley is the hiking and ski touring area of **Val S-charl** with the national park close by. The skiing area of Motta Naluns (1,250-2,785m), with its 80km of skiing pistes and 12 ski-lifts, counts among one of Switzerland's medium-sized ski areas and is further enhanced by a snow park and a piste dreams are made of; a 10 km run ending in Sent (1430m).

The Bernina Express offers a comfortable connection between Tirano and Lugano.

Lugano

Nestling beside the lake of the same name, Lugano is the Ticino's largest town and most chic resort. It's hard to know which is finer, the view from the waterfront over the shimmering blue lake or a sailor's view of the town backed up with white-tipped mountains.

The main square is **Piazza della Riforma**, covered with the tables, chairs and parasols of outdoor cafés. All sorts of activity buzz around its four corners, but the pace is still quite laid-back in this Mediterranean kind of climate. Nearby is the small **church of Santa Maria degli Angioli**, with two of Bernardino Luini's finest frescoes. **San Lorenzo cathedral**, with a Renaissance façade, has a splendid altar. On the lake shore Villa Malpensata, set in a splendid park, showcases temporary exhibitions devoted to the history of local art from the 19th to 20th centuries. The Villa Saroli (Via Stefano Franscini 9) is primarily used for administritive purposes.

In Castagnola between Lugano and the village of Gandria, you can visit the lovely Art Nouveau park of the **Villa Heleneum** with its extraordinary collection of exotic plants which thrive in the warm climate. The neoclassical villa, built in 1931, is a copy of the Petit Trianon in Versailles. It was the home of Parisian dancer, Hélène Biber, until her death in 1967, and also hosts the collections of the **Museo delle Culture** (Via Cortivo 24-28).

For exhilarating views over Lugano, the lake and the Bernese and Valais Alps, take one of the funiculars going up to **San Salvatore** or **Monte Brè**, Lugano's two conical peaks. Even better, take the train from **Capolago** to the top of Monte Generoso on the far shore of the lake opposite Lugano (via Melide and the causeway). **Melide** is home to **Swissminiatur**, with more than 120 scale models of Swiss buildings, mountains and trains.

Ferrovia Monte Generoso

During the last ice age, this mountain peak was the only one to emerge from the sea of ice, and as a result it is now home to numerous rare species of flora and fauna. The owners of the Monte Generoso railway line — the supermarket cooperative Migros — take care to stress their respect for nature and the

Ferrovia delle Centovalli:
Type: narrow-gauge electric railway
Traction: adherence
Length: 52,183 km
In service since: 1923
Tunnels: 32
Bridges and viaducts: 83

environment in the activities on offer at the summit.

In 1867, before the roads and railways were built, the **Hotel Monte Generoso Bellavista** was built on the mountaintop, its guests arriving on foot, by mule or sedan chair. Local nobles would make the journey just for the splendid view, which sweeps over the Lombard plain as far as Milan, over the alpine range from the Eiger to the Matterhorn and from the Jungfrau to Monte Rosa, with the blue lake below.

In 1886 the owner of the hotel, Dr Carlo Pasta, decided to facilitate access by building a narrow-gauge cog-wheel railway, which, after much protestation from the locals and numerous financial difficulties, was inaugurated in 1890, covering a distance of 9 km. Climbing from Capolago to Vetta, at 1,704 m (5,591 ft), the train was a resounding success, carrying over 19,000 passengers the first year. However, it eventually proved unviable and, after the two world wars, was teetering on the brink of destruction.

A white knight appeared in the form of Gottlieb Duttweiler, founder of Migros, who bought the company in 1941. The installations were renovated, the rolling stock renewed, the steam engines replaced by diesel locomotives and the ticket prices lowered. The line was electrified in 1982. Today the Monte Generoso train is the only one with two carriages for transporting people confined to wheelchairs. Bi-monthly on Sundays from June to September, special rides are organized, the train being pulled by Switzerland's oldest steam engine which dates from 1890.

Grotto. The name is derived from natural caves–*grottoes*–in which the people of Ticino originally stored wine, ham and cheese. As modern cooling and conservation methods made this form of foodstorage superfluous, many of the peasants transformed these caves into meeting places for the tasting of wine and other locally produced goods. The first authorizations to serve food and drink in the caves was given in the 19th century, and in the course of the 20th century the grotti were transformed into regular public licensed houses. The grottoes now in use are mostly no longer cave bars, but simple, traditional houses of stone, nearly always with granite tables and benches. As the main activity of the restaurant business is now aimed at tourists, most of the grotti are only open in summer.

The line is closed from November until mid- March.

At the top of the mountain you can eat in the fabulously positioned traditional restaurant, or on its panoramic terrace. Several marked walking trails, each divulging information on a specific theme such as trees or geology, lead from here. An **observatory** with a 61-cm diameter telescope was set up in 1996; it is open for public visits.

On the east esplanade of the Vetta Restaurant (10 minutes walk away) is the start of the '**Trail of planets**', a model of the planetary system reduced to the scale of 1:10,000 million and set out over 600 m (656 yd) long, in a straight line along the Swiss-Italian border. It begins with a 3-D model of the sun and continues with nine two-dimensional models from Mercury to far-off Pluto.

The karst rock of Monte Generoso is riddled with tunnels and caves; **Grotta dell'Orso** (Bear's Cave), a 30-minute walk from Vetta, was discovered in 1988. Bones from over 500 bear species which roamed the area some 30,000 to 50,000 years ago, were found there. Tickets for the guided tour are available from the ticket office at Capologo, the cafe

at the mountain's summit and also at the cave's entrance.

Around the summit you will see stone conical constructions called **nevere**; there are over 70 of these "snow silos" in the area. In medieval times the shepherds used them, packed with snow, to keep their cheese, butter and milk cool. It's said their shape inspired Swiss architect, Mario Botta.

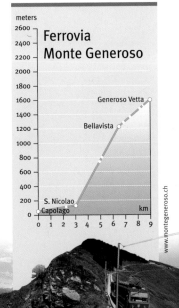

www.montegeneroso.ch

The Madonna del Sasso, high above Locarno, can be reached via the funicular.

Locarno

Locarno sits in a perfect location on the north shore of Lake Maggiore. The town owes its idyllic, almost Mediterranean atmosphere to its temperate climate and to the palms, olive and almond trees that flourish in the parks and along the lake shore.

The central point of the attractive, Italian-style town is the **Piazza Grande**, surrounded by bourgeois houses of the 18th and 19th centuries. Every summer the square is transformed into an outdoor cinema for the screenings of the **Locarno International Film Festival**.

On Piazza S. Antonio, further west, stands the Casa Rusca, a 17th-century palace housing the Municipal **Museum of Fine Arts** (Pinacoteca comunale). It houses the major part of works by French Dadaist and Surrealist Hans Arp (1886-1966) as well as exhibiting a private collection.

It is also worth visiting the **Museo Civico e Archeologico** in the Castello Visconteo, originally a 13th-century fortress which was later occupied by the confederate bailiffs.

Far above the town, reached by funicular, stands the emblem of Locarno, the 16th–17th-century **pilgrimage church of the Madonna del Sasso**. The richly decorated interior and nearby religious museum display numerous ex-voto, paintings and sculptures of great value.

The terminus of the funicular is in Orselina. From there, the cable-car takes you to Locarno's local mountain, Cardada (1,340 m), which offers great hiking and skiing. The chair-lift then carries you up to Cimetta (1,670 m). Enjoy the splendid panorama.

Ferrovia delle Centovalli

At the end of the 19th century, the authorities and economic worthies of the Ticino canton and neighbouring Italian province of Novarra tried to improve the railway links with western Switzerland and the North. The route of the line was self-imposed: it would pass by the Centovalli stretching from east to west and continue in Italy via the Valle Vigezzo. In 1912, the project for the Centovalli railway was ratified, creating the shortest liaison between the two main transalpine roads leading to the South, namely, the Gotthard and Simplon lines—as well as between the Ticino and the Valais.

Centovalli/Vigezzina: technical data
Type: narrow-gauge electric railway
Traction: adhesive
Length: 17.22 km – 32.34 km
(10.7 – 20 miles)
In service since: 1923
Tunnels: 7 – 25 / **Bridges:** 22 – 11

But several more years were to pass before the Centovalli Bahn (or the Vigezzina, as the line is called on the Italian side), could see the light of day. The engineers had to face the various technical problems caused by this wild and narrow alpine valley, on top of which came financial difficulties. Then work came to an abrupt halt because of World War I. The stretch of trans-frontier line from Locarno to Domodossola, 52 km (32 miles) long, came into service in 1923. It was managed jointly by the Ferrovie Autolinee Regionali Ticinesi (FART) and the Societá Subalpina di Imprese Ferroviarie (SSIF).

The line was modernized in the 1950s. In 1978, a storm washed away the tracks in several places on the Italian stretch and destroyed four bridges—you can still see traces of the catastrophe. The line was quickly repaired and renewed for a second time, and now travellers from the world over enjoy this romantic narrow-gauge train route with its numerous bridges and tunnels.

From Locarno to Camedo (Switzerland)

You have to go underground to board the **Centovalli** train: until the new station and 3-km-long tunnel were built in 1990, the train used to run through overground, through the traffic-congested streets. The train comes out into the light of day in the Pedemonte, as they call the region at the beginning of the Centovalli. Small vineyards alternate with old stone-roofed houses and modern apartment blocks. Unique to the valley villages in this area are

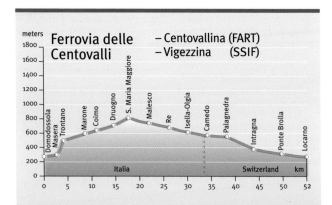

Ferrovia delle Centovalli — Centovallina (FART) — Vigezzina (SSIF)

the grotti, small rustic restaurants with pleasant shaded courtyards—good places to sample Ticino specialities such as minestrone soup and a glass of the local Merlot or Nostrano wines.

The first highlight of the journey comes at **Ponte Brolla**, at the entrance to the Centovalli. The River Maggia, which the train followed to this point, turns into its own valley. From the railway bridge, you get a splendid view over the river bed, with its strange polished rock formations, smooth pebbles and deep pools. The "Hundred Valleys", as the name Centovalli suggests, does not end directly in the main valley, but if you count all the side arms branching off to it, there are over 100.

Once past the picturesque village of Tegna, the train pulls into **Verscio**, where in 1975 the Ticino clown Dimitri set up his Teatro Dimitri, with a School for Theatre. A museum, the Museo Comico, opened in 2000. Outside the village, the church of San Fedela has a fine fresco of Christ Pantocrator painted by Antonio da Tradate around 1400. The valley narrows slowly while the deep gorges, rushing waterfalls and dizzying bridges multiply.

The principal village of Centovalli is **Intragna**, built on a rocky ledge between the Melezza and Isorno rivers, is dominated by a superb belltower, the highest in

123rf.com/Lehmann

Alluring green waters close to Ponte Brolla.

the Ticino at 69 m (226 ft). An interesting folklore museum is housed in a 17th-century patrician mansion. The railway bridge over the Isorno is of dizzying height, at 72 m (236 ft); little wonder that bungy jumpers leap off over the side. Down in the gorges, you may see the old Roman bridge.

The railway line clings to the wooded sides of the mountain, high above the Melezza. After Verdasio and Palagnedra, where the river forms a small artificial lake, you reach **Camedo**, on the frontier with Italy.

Marvellous landscapes in Centovalli and Valle Vigezzo.

www.centovalli.ch

From Camedo to Domodossola (Italy)

On the Italian side, the valley takes the name of Valle Vigezzo, the line becomes the Vigezzina, and the river the Melezzo. The next architectural highlight is the mighty **pilgrimage church of Re**. The neo-Gothic-Byzantine shrine was built in the first half of the 20th century, near the remains of an older church where a miraculous Virgin is said to have appeared in 1494, shedding tears of blood.

Past several typical Piedmontese villages, the train enters **Santa Maria Maggiore**, capital of the Valle Vigezzo and culminating point of the line at 830 m (272 ft) high. Have an aperitivo on the picturesque piazza and admire the handsome palazzi surrounding it, bearing witness to the town's golden age. The small but fascinating **Museo dello Spazzacamino**, is behind the Town Hall. It documents the fate of countless children of the **Vigezzo, Centovalli and Onsernone valleys** sent to Milan, Turin or Paris in the 18th century to earn a meagre living as chimney sweeps. Installed in a 19th century villa, the **Pinacoteca Rossetti Valentini** displays a collection of paintings from the Rossetti Valentini School of Art, founded in 1878, which lends the Valley Vigezzo its nickname 'Valley of the Painters'. Today, **Santa Maria Maggiore** is a popular sports resort.

The train then passes slowly through varied countryside of chestnut plantations and charming old villages, some of which are abandoned, proof of the way this valley has struggled against the consequences of emigration.

At **Trontano** the train begins an abrupt descent—of great interest to anyone fascinated by the techniques of railway engineering—to Domodossola, which lies in the light of the Toce plain. Several tight curves, bridges and terraced walls in the midst of the vines permit the track to drop down in altitude as far as **Masera**. There, the train takes a huge curve before arriving at Domodossola.

Domodossola

Since Roman times, this North Italian town has been an important communications crossroads, and its famous Saturday market, held on the pretty **Piazza del Mercato**, attracts buyers from far and wide. Wander through the streets and discover the 15th- to 17th-century palaces, see the imposing **Collegial Church of St Gervase and St Protase**, or sit on a café's terrace to soak up the Italian atmosphere. Nine sacred mountains, '**Sacri Monti**' in Piedmont and Lombardi, including the **Sacro Monte di Domodossola**, became Unesco listed in 2003. These paths of devotion pass through groups of chapels built amongst great beauty.

Hearty Swiss food; Rösti are made of grated potatoes fried in butter.

DINING OUT

Keeping true to its tradition of playing international host, Switzerland, though small, has space enough to accommodate the various regional specialities as well as global cuisines. Ethnic differences are reflected in the range of local dishes, in Swiss-French, Swiss-German and Swiss-Italian styles.

Starters

One of the most popular appetizers, *Bündnerfleisch* or *viande séchée* consists of paper-thin slices of dried meat served with gherkins and pickled onions, or as one of an assortment of cold cuts in an *assiette valaisanne*. Lucerne has a favourite starter in bread soup *(Brotsuppe)* whilst a nutritious soup made with barley is waiting for you in Granbünden.

A speciality Ticino soup is the minestrone (vegetable soup), but don't miss the *antipasti*, too: vegetables marinated in olive oil, salami or *bruschetta*–toasted bread with diced tomato, often garlic-spiced.

Main Dishes

The limpid waters of the country's rivers and lakes produce such outstanding freshwater fish as pike, trout, whitefish, char and perch, both from Lake Geneva. The latter is served fried with a tartar sauce, while the char *(omble chevalier)* is served poached with a *sauce hollandaise* or with melted butter.

Switzerland can boast roughly 450 types of sausage. In the French-speaking region the best-known ones are *saucisse aux choux* (incorporating cabbage), *saucisson vaudois* and *boutefas*; but if you're in German Switzerland, you should look for *Schüblig* and *Bratwurst* from pork or veal, served sizzling hot with a potato salad.

A Zurich speciality found all over the country, *Geschnetzeltes Kalbfleisch* or *émincé zurichois*, consists of sautéed slivers of veal and mushrooms in a rich cream sauce. The habitual garnish is *Rösti*, a tasty version of grated fried potatoes whose original home was German Switzerland but today it is eaten everywhere. Bern includes it all in the *Bernerplatte*, a selection of sausages, ham, bacon, pork chops and boiled beef served on a heap of sauerkraut, beans and of course, potatoes.

The coveted saffron of the Valais village of Mund has been registered as an *appellation d'origine contrôlée* (AOC) since 2004; the reason why Ticino is not the only region in which you will find saffron rice any more.

Ticino is famous for its stufato alla Luganese (braised beef or pork) and braised rabbit (coniglio), served most often with polenta. And in Poschiavo, try the *pizzoccheri*—buckwheat dumplings.

Dessert

Have a slice of fruit tart (*Obstkuchen* or *tarte aux fruits*). In the French cantons, tarts are also made with a reduction of wine (*tarte au vin cuit*). More typical of Gruyere or the Pays d'En haut and canton of Bern are the meringues (made up with egg whites,

Fondue and Raclette. No visit to Switzerland is complete without one meal of *Fondue*. It tastes best when eaten with a group of friends seated around the earthenware pot *(caquelon)* and dipping cubes of bread into a heated mixture of melted cheese and white wine. The *fondue* mixture differs from one region to another using different local cheeses. The most widely spread variation is *moitié-moitié*, half *gruyère*, half *vacherin*.

Raclette, too, is a melted-cheese dish. For a genuine *raclette*, the cut surface of half a wheel of cheese is heated and then scraped onto the plate with a boiled potato in its skin and spicy pickled vegetables. Another popular way of serving is with small portions of cheese in a special little *raclette* oven. A dry white wine is recommended both for fondue and raclette, hot black tea or a glass of *Kirsch* (cherry brandy).

baked in the oven and garnished with double cream). Try baked apples in vanilla sauce or Kirschtorte, a rich gateau soaked in kirsch, and *Rüeblitorte* (carrotcake). Graubünden also boasts a toothachingly rich walnut pie from the Engadine called *Tuorta da Nusch*. Ticino appreciates a foamy *zabaglione (sabayon)*, beaten eggs spiked with Marsala as the perfect end to a meal.

No exploration of Swiss cuisine would be complete without the mention of cheese, even as a desert. It may take a dedicated amateur to go through all the varieties, but you can begin by trying the better-known ones. In the Canton de Vaud ask for a "*tomme*", in Gruyère taste a mature gruyère and in the Mattertal (Valais) or in Granbüten enjoy goats' cheese and in Ticino a pyramida "zincarlin" which is stocked in the caves of Monte Generoso.

Drinks

Besides the country's outstanding drinking water and the large range of quality beers on offer, there are many fine local wines to sample. Most of the vineyards are located in the canton of Geneva, Vaud, Valais and Ticino, but wine is also produced in almost all the other cantons.

For some years now, the widely produced Chasselas,

Huber/Simeone

www.la-gruyere.ch

An authentic Walliser plate with regional specialities. | Meringues; a sweet seduction.

Gamay and Pinot grapes have been supplemented and even in some cases replaced, in both Vaud and Valais, by other super grape varieties. Today, top –quality red wines are produced with grapes such as Cornalin, Humagne Rouge and Syrah, whilst whites are produced with Petite Arvine, Humagne Blanc, Amigne and Chardonnay. In Ticino, soft, red Merlot wines tend to predominate, whilst whites are generally produced with Chardonnay or Sauvignon.

Crayons from Caran d'Ache are a high-quality, Swiss branded product.

CARAN d'ACHE · SWISS MA

CARAN d'ACHE · SWISS MA

CARAN d'ACHE · SWISS MA

CARAN d'ACHE · SWISS M

CARAN d'ACHE · SWISS M

CARAN d'ACHE · SWISS

Caran d'Ache SA, Thônex-Genève

SHOPPING

The quality of Swiss goods is comfortingly solid, however expensive they may be. Everything is made to last, and is generally in good taste. Even if some of the prices take your breath away, you will also find plenty of attractive, moderately priced choices.

Clothing

In the realm of clothing, there is everything from elegant high-fashion shoes, through embroidery and lace, blouses and flannel or cotton edelweiss-patterned shirts, down to cotton handkerchiefs, witty T-shirts and socks. Traditional costumes, waistcoats for polar temperatures, pyjamas or underwear with Swiss motifs.

Children

For children there are dolls dressed in various regional costumes, beautiful jigsaw puzzles and wooden toys, rucksacks and most popular of all, the great range of boxes of colourful pencils and crayons, easy to pack.

Cosmetics

Swiss cosmetic products are often organic and produced as naturally as possible; for example skin creams from Valais extract of apricot, edelweiss essences for taut skin or even marmot ointment for muscular ailments.

Kitchen-, tableware and Gourmet products

You'll find a great range of matching table linen and kitchencloths. Buy the appropriate utensils and dishes for fondue and raclette—and the right cheeses and wines, too. Look for herbal teas made from hand-picked plants and dried Alpine herbs. In Val Poschiavo, you will find the region's special durum wheat pasta noodles. For traditional sausages and dried meats, head for Salsiz, Bündnerfleisch and Steinbockwurst—they do travel well, but you can also get them vacuum-sealed.

Craftwork

The folkloric or edelweiss patterned tablecloths and place settings are irresistible as are the prints of paper cut-outs known as poyas which often portray the procession of cows up to the Alpine meadows for the summer months, as well as many other designs. Galleries also sell real

The Wonders of Mechanical Music. The musical box was invented in 1796 by a Geneva clock-maker who wanted in this way to increase the value of pocket watches. In 1865, Charles Reuge founded in Sainte-Croix in the Swiss Jura the Reuge Musical Box Factory — which to this days still possesses the monopoly in the manufacture of mechanical songbirds and musical boxes. In the second half of the 19th century, the musical box industry in Sainte-Croix experienced an enormous boom. Charles Reuge's grandson, Guido, headed the company from 1930 for more than 60 years. For lack of a family heir, the factory had to be sold in 1988 to do justice to investments and productivity. The challenge remains to keep the art of this handicraft going with new designs and creations. To this day, the unique musical mechanism is still heard around the world. Whether it be songbirds, simple musical boxes or luxury musical clocks, the sounds still bring pleasure not only to collectors but continue to fascinate all who value the fantastic link between machine, sound and art.

Reuge SA, Sainte-Croix

hand-painted poyas on long cross-sections of wood, which are usually nailed above farmhouse doors. These come mainly from Château d'Oex and Gstaad. You will find a host of talented wood carvers in Brienz.

Sporting Goods

This land of hiking and skiing is the place to fit yourself out with a great range of summer and winter clothes and equipment. A good tip: buy your winter goods in the summer, the prices are better.

Sweetmeats

You will of course not forget the Swiss chocolates, but in summer these are best eaten on the spot, rather than left to melt in your luggage. The last chance for chocolate is at the airport; you will find a large range of Pralinés, usually presented rather beautifully.

Otherwise, Engadine nut cake or Lucerne Birnbrot (literally "pear bread", a kind of Strudel) are both delicious — and travel well when packed properly.

Pocket Knives

Besides the many other blades and ingenious tools, the latest gadget to be added to the famous Swiss Army Knife is a USB flash drive. (To avoid confiscation at the security check, pack knives safely in your checked-in luggage). Also available in silver, gold or set with diamonds!

Watches and Clocks

Favourite purchases are wristwatches - famous makes like Swatch in "fun" quartzes and sport versions as well as priceless bejewelled models. You can also buy attractive fob watches on chains, the dial and case adorned with pastoral scenes or edelweiss.

Shop at recognized stores and check the guarantee on your goods. Cuckoo clocks can be bought in the souvenir shops. The famous Swiss Federal Railways clock—or in miniature as a watch—can be bought at the larger stations and branches of the Schweizer Heimatwerk, notably at the airports.

The Heimatwerk offers a lot of very nice products from all over Switzerland and is located in the Duty Free Zone—a good way to utilise the last of your Swiss francs by buying a few souvenirs or gifts!

Swiss Quality products: cotton shirts with an Edelweiss motif, a variety of watches, the classical Swiss pocket knife and delicious Swiss chocolate.

istockphoto.com/Opyd

istockphoto.com/haveseen

istockphoto.com/van Caspel

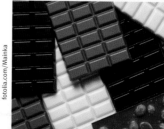
fotolia.com/Mainka

THE HARD FACTS

Buying your ticket

If you haven't purchased a rail pass or bought your ticket on-line, you can obtain one from a touch-screen machine at the station, or from the ticket office. You can obtain information on daily tickets, special offers and reduced price tickets from the ticket office too.

Accompanied children of under 6 years old can travel free of charge, those from 6 to 16 yrs are subject to a half -fare fee.

From home you can buy an *OnlineTicket* from the online ticket shop Ticket Shop CFF which you can either print off or send to your mobile phone in the form of an *MMS Ticket*. This last option is only available for certain links.

If you have a smart phone, the free application Mobile CFF permits you to buy tickets whenever you like and to consult the latest timetables.

You must have a valid ticket before you get on the train. The inspectors can sell tickets (and you can pay with a credit card) but you will also be fined. If you have a ticket but get on the wrong train, you will have to pay a fine plus the price of your mistaken journey. If you have a second-class ticket and decide to travel in first class, you can pay the difference when the inspector comes round.

You will find information on the different services available (business or silent carriages, internet access, buffet cars and bicycle storage) by consulting the timetables, under the specific headings. or by looking online at www.cff.ch under 'stations and services'.

Climate

Thanks to the protective barrier of the Alps and the variable altitudes, the Swiss climate differs regionally. In general, the region north of the Alps is subject to Atlantic and Continental influences, with pleasantly warm summers and chilly winters. South of the Alps, the climate is Mediterranean, with warm to hot summers and mild winters. Major differences in altitude between separate regions add to differences in weather conditions.

Average temperatures in summer range from 18 to 28°C (62.4 to 82.4°F) and in winter from −2 to 7°C (28.4 to 44.6°F). Up to date weather information is available by telephone: 162 for the weather report and 163 for road conditions.

Clothing

Essentials include a good, light-weight water and windproof coat, a comfortable pair of walking shoes and sunglasses. Pack a fleece and a swimsuit and when getting dressed, start with a t-shirt and layer up!

Currency

The Swiss currency is the franc (Franken in German, franco in Italian), abbreviated CHF, SFr or frs. It is divided into 100 centimes (Rappen in German, centesimi in Italian). International credit cards are widely used as a means of payment and there are plenty of ATMs for cash withdrawals. Euros are widely accepted in shops, hotels and restaurants.

Average temperatures in summer range from 18 to 28°C (62.4 to 82.4°F) and in winter from −2 to 7°C (28.4 to 44.6°F).

Emergencies

Medical services: Telephone 144, Police 117, Fire department 118.

»Fly Rail Baggage«

With some airlines, you can check in your luggage (not bulky items) at your departure airport and have it delivered to your final Swiss destination and vice versa. In some stations you will also receive your boarding card and seat assignment for the plane. Details on www.sbb.ch.

Handicapped travellers

Special seats are reserved near the doors of certain carriages for people in wheelchairs. At the time of printing, over 150 stations are equipped with wheelchair "mobilifts" or ramps.

For a member of staff to meet you at your departure and arrival stations, phone 2 hours in advance to the Call Center Handicap,

open daily 6 a.m.–10 p.m.,
0800 007 102 (toll-free),
or fax 0512 257 090;

from abroad dial +41 512 257 150; 24 hours in advance by e-mail mobil@sbb.ch.

Taxis

Taxis are metered; the fares are expensive by UK standards. Cabs are available at most railway stations (or you can telephone for one from the station). They can't be flagged down in the street. Taxi drivers are usually tipped; you can round up the fare.

Tipping

A service charge of 15% is included in all hotel and restaurant bills, as well as in taxi fares and at the hairdressers. It is customary to round up the bill, and in restaurants some people leave a larger tip. Chambermaids should be tipped at least SFr 1.50 per day; offer porters either a 2 or 5 franc coin.

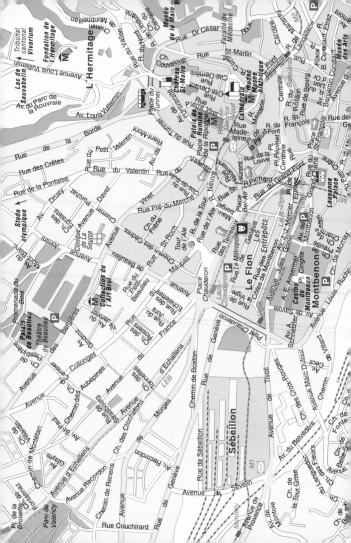

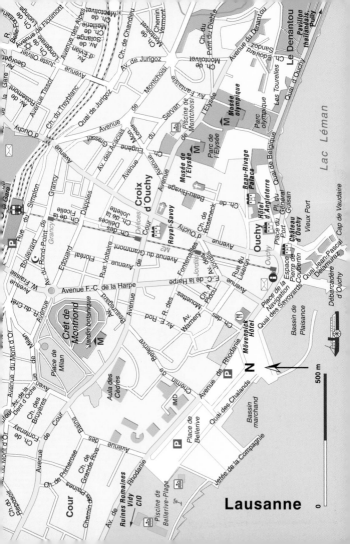

Lausanne

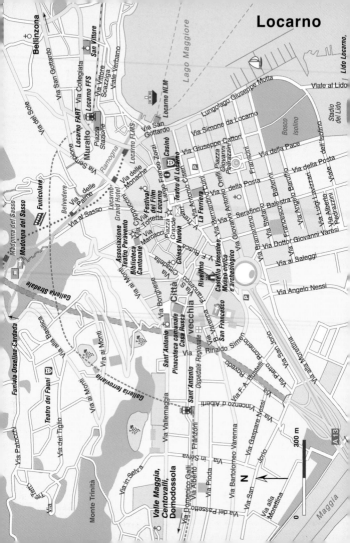

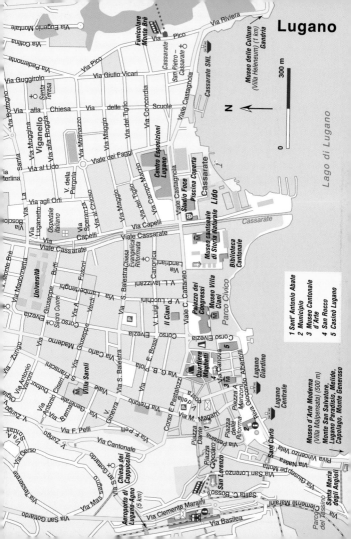

Lucerne
Old Town

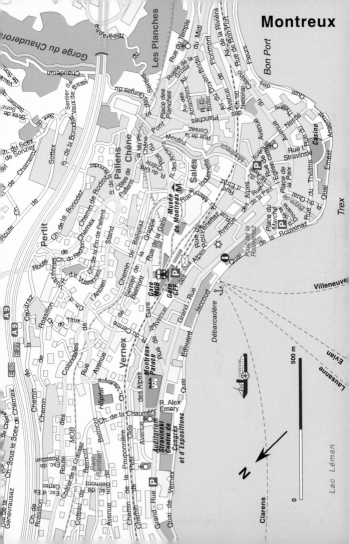

Editors
Petronella Greenhalgh
Eleonora Di Campli

Original text
M. Lukas-Grossenbacher

Design
Karin Palazzolo

Layout
Luc Malherbe
Matias Jolliet

Photo credits
P. 1: Jungfrau-Bahn (train)
P. 2: Suisse Tourisme (clock),
Rhätische Bahn/Max Galli
(Engadine landscape),
Lenk-Simmental Tourismus AG
(cow)

Maps
JPM Publications,
Mathieu Germay

Translation:
Jack Altman

Copyright © 2013, 2005
JPM Publications S.A.
12, avenue William-Fraisse,
1006 Lausanne, Switzerland
information@jpmguides.com
http://www.jpmguides.com/

Every care has been taken to
verify the information in the
guide, but the publisher cannot
accept responsibility for any
errors that may have occurred.
If you spot an inaccuracy or a
serious omission, please let
us know.

Printed in Germany
15822.00.14793
Edition 2013